Advance praise for *Open your Mind*

Our world organisations are more complex than ever before. Unravelling complexity and making sense of it requires leaders to reflect and think critically. However, leaders are taught to quickly move into action to achieve results. They are often so focused on answers that they forget to ask the important questions. This book provides a valuable resource for leaders and gives them excellent tools for learning the core competency of critical thinking.

Diane L. Dixon, Ed.D., Managing Principal,
D. Dixon & Associates, LLC

George Eliot once said that it is never too late to be what you might have been. Sofo takes an essentially creative approach to showing us how to think critically. His seven keys are easy and useful ways to open our minds to respecting other views and to generating inspired alternatives. Critical thinking is indeed our ability to maximise our capacity which means we will be able to create powerful individual and organisational improvements. Sofo shows that critical and creative thinking are skills that can be mastered by everyone.

Michael Marquardt, Professor of HRD, George Washington University

The necessity and ability to look at aspects of our lives with fresh perspectives and open minds is made more urgent in an increasingly complicated and interrelated world. This book provides useful tools to help us see with new eyes and think with new minds.

Andrew Simon, M.Ed., Adjunct Lecturer, University of Canberra

Dr Sofo has managed, in a non-academic and creative way, to address the often one-dimensional way we see 'critical thinking'. As the primary function which shapes our feeling, moods and behaviour, this insight is particularly useful for people in all walks of life, especially in the executive coaching arena. I will add this to my armoury of tools on coaching senior executives in the public sector.

Lindy Bryant, Executive Coach, Mediator and
Director of Yellow Edge Pty Ltd

Unless and until we change the way we think, and engage in critical thinking we cannot bring about effective change. This is a skill we should be assessing in evaluating talent and/or be teaching this to individuals in all roles. This book can serve as a key link between 'how to' and 'can do'.

Marilyn Repinski, HR First/Independent Consultant

Great book! It opens your mind to thinking about issues in a different light and being creative when all is well rather than focusing on problem solving. It has encouraged me to empower my staff and stimulate their creativity. It's like stepping outside yourself and looking at the way you do things with a fresh set of eyes.

Arthur Roufogalis, General Manager,
Canberra Labor Club Group

Brilliant stuff . . . I am most impressed by the easy-to-follow approach to embrace critical thinking, rather than just the standard theoretical/conceptual text. This book will contribute significantly to advancing the practice of such an important area.

Stephen Hewitt, Master of Community Ed. (HRD),
HRD Consultant

Fresh, important, and useful.

Linda Tobey, PhD, author of The Integrity Moment

Few people have the ability to leave this world a better place through all they say and do. Dr Sofo not only manages to achieve this, but also inspires in others the desire to do the same.

Michelle Berzins,
Australian Competition and Consumer Commission

Contents

Acknowledgements

In 1985, my family and I came to Canberra, Australia's capital, so I could take responsibility for the Special Education courses at Signadou College, now the Australian Catholic University. One of my first resolves was to assist student-teachers to increase their awareness of the importance of thinking in the classroom. I had the opportunity of studying with Matthew Lipman and Ann Sharpe from Montclaire State College in New Jersey, USA. Matt is the inventor of the Philosophy for Children program. He helped me greatly to consolidate my approach to teaching the art of thinking.

Nobody ever achieves anything on their own. During the various stages of writing this book I have called on my students at the University of Canberra, colleagues and friends to read the manuscript or parts of it and to offer a reaction and advice. I have found them all most obliging and helpful and wish to thank them sincerely for their energetic engagement with me on this project on thinking critically which is a passion we share. We are all in the field of wanting to help people achieve their full potential and it is this unity of purpose that enables us to assist each other so generously. Thank you all: Mary, my partner; Daniel Sofo, son and manager, Café Pacific; Andrew Simon, adjunct lecturer, University of Canberra; Bob McAlister, student and colleague; Lindy Bryant, colleague, Director, Yellow Edge Pty Ltd; Nola Mostyn, Australian

Maritime Safety Authority; Eleanor Waight, student, HRD program; Mario Raich, consultant, Raich Limited; Coral Love, student, Master of HRD; Deanne Ranyard, student, tutor, University of Canberra; Michelle Berzins, research assistant, Australian Competition and Consumer Commission; Stephen Hewitt, student and HRD consultant, United Nations; Eugene Clark, Head of Law, University of Canberra; Roger Dean, Vice-Chancellor, University of Canberra; Linda Tobey, author of *The Integrity Moment*; Marilyn Rapinski, HR First/Independent Consultant; Michael Marquardt, Professor, George Washington University; Falinda Geerling, Writing Specialist, Spring Arbor University, USA; Robert Alan Black, creativity guru; Arthur Roufogalis and Glenn Wallace, colleagues and executives, Canberra Labor Club Group; Diane L. Dixon, Ed.D., D. Dixon & Associates, LLC; John McCaffrey, doctoral student, Department of Science and Technology; Lee Dudley, student, University of Canberra; Janelle Wallace, student and mathematics teacher; Deborah Koehle, editor, USA.

I also want to acknowledge the influence of my father, Agostino, who encouraged me as a child and young man to learn to my full capacity, and my mother, Carmela, who still tells me to 'love everyone' (*voleteve bene con tutti*) and to my extended family and five sons, Daniel, Adam, James, Olivier and Charles, who are always supportive.

Francesco.Sofo@canberra.edu.au
University of Canberra
1 July 2003

About the author

Dr Francesco Sofo convenes the graduate professional development education courses and the Master of Human Resource Development (HRD) at the University of Canberra, Australia. This is his fourth book. His textbook, *HRD: Perspectives, Roles and Practice Choices* is used in Australian Universities and in Indonesian and Chinese University graduate courses. His research, community work and consultancy focus on ways to improve individuals, groups, organisations and communities. Francesco loves people, learning, music, languages and life!

Introduction

Lucy: Do you think anybody ever really changes?
Linus: I've changed a lot in the last year.
Lucy: I mean for the better.
—Charles M. Schulz, cartoonist

If you accept my invitation to read this book, you'll enter a different world. You'll find you notice everyday things in a different way. You'll identify and question the things you take for granted. You'll enhance your mental capacity and you'll develop a genuine appreciation for others, for your environment and for yourself. If you heed the advice I offer you'll learn to open your mind to thinking critically. And thinking critically benefits all human beings because it enables us to create a more peaceful world, to have a more balanced life and to look forward to a more prosperous future.

More than ever there is increased pressure on us to learn and adapt. We are aware of just how much technology and communication advances continue to create unprecedented opportunities for us and, simultaneously, how they increase pressure on us to be innovative and to be the first with an edge. There is hardly any time to slack off or relax. Well, in this book I am intensifying the pressure. I am urging you to get on top of this thing vital to progress, to get that edge, to generate alternatives and to achieve a more focused approach. Get into thinking critically. Why? Because then you will be able to move to a greater level of independence and freedom of thought and action. You will also realise that what is needed in the twenty-first century more than any time before is for all of us to achieve a healthy interdependence. Thinking critically in groups, communities and organisations, locally and globally, provides our most highly evolved edge to the future. The stark imperative now is to grow and develop together, or else become obsolete!

If you love your life exactly the way it is and don't want anything to change, thinking critically is not for you. If you're perfectly happy with your personal and professional relationships, thinking critically is not for you. If you are a model of efficiency at work, thinking critically may not be for you unless you can see that the improvement process is never-ending and that there is always room for enhancing efficiency. If nothing in the wide world puzzles or entrances you, then thinking critically at its best will only be a pastime.

If, however, you want to stretch the boundaries of your perception, to enhance your mental capacity and to perceive the invisible in what you look at every day, then read this book and turn the keys to improve your capacity to think divergently and creatively, to think critically. In this book I urge you to open your mind and dare to think differently.

As a teacher, I have always recognised the need for children to think for themselves. In theory, the purpose of education is to foster this independence in thinking. It's generally understood that developing basic analytical skills in the classroom is an important way to develop the capacity for creativity and self-expression, which in turn help us to attain our aspirations. This has not always been my experience. For example, I have observed many a classroom teacher constantly questioning students in a closed-ended fashion, limiting their responses to single answers rather than encouraging initiative and divergence in thinking. Many teachers too often create barriers and establish expectations in student responses that inhibit their creativity and self-expression. As a result of my observations it became my passion to help students to improve their thinking skills, and I try to incorporate my methods into every course I teach.

I found six simple methods encouraged students to think for themselves. These methods require me to:

1. Expect students to plan and prepare for learning before the lesson began through identifying what they hoped to gain and learn from the lesson, a technique I call 'pre-flection'.
2. Allow students to do more structured talking by bouncing ideas off each other rather than the discussions being teacher–student centred. This meant me talking less and listening more so that my role increasingly became one of facilitator for the discussion.
3. Ask open-ended questions to help students explore ideas.
4. Refrain from agreeing or disagreeing with student responses to encourage them to evaluate their responses and reasoning.
5. Re-direct students' uncertainties to other students rather than myself, which enabled further exploration and conversation, with an openness to different perspectives and a healthy challenge of ideas. This also enabled people to seek good reasons for their position.
6. Encourage students to discuss in small groups their emotions and feelings about the discussion, to identify the key concepts or ideas they found new or interesting and to decide how they might grow or develop from the lesson. I called this three-step group-reflection technique 'ECG'—Emotions, Concepts and Growth. Students became accustomed to doing an ECG at the end of lessons and briefly reporting on it at the next lesson.

The six methods attend to critical reflection before, during and after a lesson, ensuring students are encouraged to use their initiative and to think cooperatively and for themselves. Using these methods, I found that students' scores on reasoning tests greatly improved. The techniques encouraged both adults and children to share ideas and to be more open to different ways of thinking. At the same time, I began work as a human resource development consultant to businesses, chiefly focusing on how managers could improve their own thinking to develop themselves, their people and their organisation. In this big, grown-up world, I found many workplaces mirrored the repressive atmosphere of those schools that stifled thinking in individuals. I discovered that managers expected a lot from their staff but didn't always encourage them to share their unique points of view and personal insights or give independent assessments. Employees, students, class teachers, managers and others need strong and persistent support to advance their thinking capacity so they have the courage to question assumptions and beliefs. The qualities that are most desirable can be achieved only when people think for themselves.

Thinking critically liberates you to look deeper and to consider alternatives. The following story illustrates this point.

There once was a man called John, walking alone through the country towards the town. Another man, Nathaniel, was walking out of the town with his donkey. Nathaniel stopped and said to John, 'Excuse me, sir, but has your donkey ever had colic?'

'Why, yes', replied John.

'Could you tell me then what did you do?'

'I gave him a good dose of turpentine', replied John.

'Ah, thank you.'

'It is my pleasure', replied John. They each resumed their own journey.

A few days later the two men met again on the edge of town, close to the spot where they had their first exchange. Neither of them had a donkey this time. Nathaniel was again the first to speak.

'Hello, again. Do you remember me? You told me your donkey had colic and that you gave him turps. Where is your donkey?'

'My donkey died after I gave him the dose of turps', replied John. 'Where's your donkey?'

'I am sad to say he died too, after I gave him a good dose of turps.' And they continued their journey.

By not questioning John about his cure Nathaniel has suffered a loss. He didn't think critically beyond the given. Wisdom is the capacity to know what to ask when.

Everyday we make decisions that must follow basic principles and one of those principles is, 'do no harm'. Some cures do more harm than the complaint, as seen in the above story. Some forms of education do more damage than the original state of ignorance— the cure can be worse than the disease. For example, a company experiencing a cash-flow crisis may choose to sell more to existing customers without broadening the customer base as a quick fix. Quick fixes tend to be short-term, even though they may be effective. Eventually the existing customers will have too much product and will stop buying. The better solution may have been to both sell more to existing customers and broaden the customer base to open up new markets.

It is also important when thinking critically to spot the underlying parameters and structures of a situation to uncover leverage points through which you can question the event. Let go of the notion that cause and effect are close in time and space and see what happens. Temporarily abandon thinking in snapshots and learn to think in terms of connected change processes. Locate leverage by identifying how many seemingly contradictory things can improve over time.

Thinking critically may not appeal to some educators or bosses because it is not a quick fix! It is a long-term investment in realising your mental capacity. To some it may be such an effort that they think they are chiselling away at granite with a toothpick! But the rewards are far too great to not think critically.

What *is* thinking critically?

> Do not follow where the path may lead. Go instead where
> there is no path and leave a trail of your own.
> —Anon

Thinking critically is about *stopping to reconsider what you take for granted.* It means re-evaluating your habits to improve the way you do things.

Thinking critically is *a journey of exploration*. It is about re-discovering something you already know. It will take you back to where you started so that you will understand in a new way.

Thinking critically is *a shift in perspective*, even if it is just a very small shift. It is about increasing your own awareness of how you think, letting go of strongly held beliefs, and creating a new mental model, a new mindset.

Thinking critically is *learning to see with new eyes*. Marcel Proust once said that 'the real voyage of discovery consists not in seeking new landscapes, but in having new eyes'. You can go further than this because, as mentioned above, thinking critically is also about seeing your own irrationally held prejudices with clearer vision.

Who's it for?

Everyone and anyone

Thinking critically isn't just for intellectuals, leaders and creative artists. It's for anyone who wants to improve their life and their productivity so they can participate more actively in the life of their community. Anyone who wants to become more aware and who has a curiosity about life and a desire to be a fully functioning human being has the capacity for critical thought. If you have the ability to focus on an issue and a willingness to start asking questions about it, then you have the capacity to think critically.

Often the need to rethink an issue comes from a bad life experience. But thinking critically doesn't have to start with pain. A desire for new knowledge and a sense of adventure can also be cogent stimulators of the need to think critically. In fact, this is the best time to begin to think critically because there is no pressure to fix the things that have gone wrong. When your business or organisation is at its peak and its profits are soaring, this is an excellent time to plan and be creative. The best results of thinking critically occur in good times. And thinking critically during the good times can help you avoid or, better, cope with trauma if it occurs.

Leonardo da Vinci once observed that iron rusts from disuse. Stagnant water also loses its purity and in cold weather becomes frozen. Similarly, inaction saps the vitality of the mind. Thinking critically is an indispensable activity for enlivening the mind and preventing it from disintegrating.

As a skill, thinking critically is something you need to master for yourself but you don't need to master it on your own.

Groups

Some of the most potent outcomes of thinking critically can occur when groups of people engage in the process together, offering a diversity of perspectives and challenges. Within a group others may ask you questions about things you take for granted, about aspects of your experience, about the way you think about problems and about any other things that occur to them from within their own mental framework. In this way others can act as a mirror for you to see yourself more clearly and to realise that, while we may share many experiences, we process them in different ways. As individuals we can also inspire and encourage each other.

While we cannot learn directly from experiences we do not have, we can learn from each others' experiences through observing, listening and questioning. Learning through observation is effective because it can open our senses to being receptive to the whole process. Being an observer need not be only a passive activity. In fact, when we observe, whether we like it or not, we *are* participants of the behaviour we observe and through thinking critically we can choose what we might do in response.

Someone open to thinking critically is a person who risks asking the 'dumb' questions and encourages others to explore fundamental issues. Such a thinker has a high regard for cooperative inquiry, openness and honesty of feelings. In group discussions, wisdom and commonsense are valued over smugness or being clever. Humility is an important attitude to cultivate in pursuing critical analysis.

Businesses

If you're a business manager and you encourage employees to think critically, then everyone's contributions become part of the solution in some way. If everyone's contributions are given a fair hearing,

whether they are eventually incorporated or rejected for good reasons, you foster a sense of freedom, a sense of confidence and a safe
sense of control in the present societal climate of uncertainty.
Thinking critically engenders participation and feelings of belong-
ing rather than domination and alienation.

It is a mistake to focus only on our own position as then we
have little sense of responsibility for the results produced when
all the positions with the business interact. Responsibilities extend
beyond the boundaries of a single position or a single person.
A willingness to accept our role as being both a single entity and
a part of a greater sum is essential. Results come from team efforts.
There is a story about a cricketer playing backstop who dropped
three should-be catches. He threw off his gloves and stormed off
the field protesting, 'No one can catch a ball in that field'. For some,
there is always someone else to blame—our fellow players, the other
side, the umpire or the rules—but we need to be able to straddle the
boundary between us and others in order to solve problems.

In business being pro-active is seen as the antidote to being reac-
tive. But acting against forces in others may not be a pro-active action.
For example, it is not necessarily useful to be pro-active when
conversing with people who have been subjected to domestic
violence. In these situations it is inappropriate to tell such a person
what to do or to offer advice on what is best for them, especially
when they are not even seeking advice. The danger with this type
of pro-activity is that it pushes your own values and judgements onto
others; it assumes that your own beliefs of what is best is in fact
'best'; it does not encourage the other person to do what is right for
them in their own time; it discourages the person from taking
responsibility and ownership for their decisions and it does not
value the person's ability to make decisions. Further, in these situations being pro-active may mean that we stick to our own agendas
and achieve our predetermined outcomes at the expense of doing
what was asked of us in the first place. When we anticipate the
unspoken word at the expense of acting upon the unspoken word
we are being inappropriately pro-active. When we anticipate the
unspoken word while acting upon the spoken word we are closer to
acting appropriately.

The essence of being pro-active is seeing how we contribute to our own problems. Being pro-active results from the way we think critically about our own contribution to the work team, not from an emotional reaction. Thinking critically dissipates the illusion of taking charge.

In a world of rapid changes in communication and technology, you can create a second order of change—a change in the way you do things and how you relate to others—in your life and in business. Thinking critically enables you to expand the full capabilities of your mind, giving you the potential to implement dramatic change in your (business) practice. The key tool for a prosperous future for any person or organisation is thinking cooperatively and critically.

How do I do it?

Open up your creative side

One of the ways you can learn to think critically is to tap into your creative side. This involves looking at ideas from different perspectives and disciplines. Understanding other people's areas of expertise can open you up to unusual options, and taking an interest in the unfamiliar can bring insights when you least expect it. For example, to be creative you simply take a statement you hear and identify just how much substance there is behind it. You can do this by asking, 'What if this assumption was not true?'

You can ask many 'What if?' questions about any statement. The 'What if?' tool starts you thinking critically as you are asking for possibilities—and you are being creative! Use 'What if?' to challenge *any* aspect of what you hear, such as information about quantity, timeframe, strategy, functions, particular features, relationships between people and objects, location, reasons or cause–effect among others. For example, 'What if there was more/less/not enough/none/too much?' 'What if it happens at a different time/place/never happens/already happened/happens differently?' The important thing is to ask, and without a doubt, you will get alternative views. The simple 'What if?' will bring instant exploration of the issue and it will help you sharpen your focus and grasp missed details and observations! 'What if?' *opens your mind* to alternative ways of seeing and thinking.

Break the rules and win

Thinking critically will help you to relax the controls, the mechanisms that keep your actions and outputs within predetermined limits. Thinking critically may inspire you to invent new systems to suit your own insights. This is a positive step, not a negative activity. In business, breaking the rules means doing something different and this in itself is a competitive act.

In many respects sudden inspiration seems like commonsense in conditions of necessity, such as using a twig to retrieve your keys from the drain, using a small coin instead of a screwdriver or tying your belt or shoe-lace around your limb to stop the blood circulation. Velcro was discovered when thistles got stuck in a man's socks— he turned a bothersome experience into a useful and profitable commodity. The roll-on deodorant was adapted from the ballpoint pen. The idea of camouflage for World War II tanks came from Picasso's art. Drive-in theatres led to drive-in takeaway, which then led to drive-in banks. Self-service petrol led to *Car Lovers*, a service where you wash your own car. Now you can even cook your own food at some restaurants.

How to navigate this book

This book is organised into two parts, the seven keys of thinking critically and thinking about thinking. Each part concentrates on ways to open your mind up to difference; to observe what you take for granted in new ways and to notice more detail as well as larger perspectives. In other words, each part helps you to step closer to reality as well as to step further back so you can comprehend and appreciate things in new ways. Opening your mind consists of processes you should engage in for the whole of your life.

The seven keys discussed in the first part of the book introduce you to seven different strategies for using your capacity to comprehend. The seven different approaches are arranged in a dynamic model called the spinning hourglass because I want to emphasise the importance of movement in your thinking. Each key can be used separately or in combination with one or more of the other keys. The spinning hourglass is designed to help you remember three sets of keys. The three keys surrounding the three sides of one swirl on the spinning hourglass focus on you specifically improving your personal capacity to enjoy and question and to encourage thinking in different ways. The hub of the spinning hourglass, the open group, represents group skills of thinking critically where you get to test your ideas with others before you set out on your own. The three keys surrounding the three sides of the other swirl of the spinning hourglass are more daring and challenging, requiring you to step out of your comfort zone with others and to show yourself to be thinking in different ways by offering different perspectives.

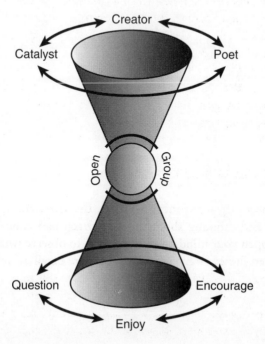

The second part of the book deals in detail with some essential elements of thinking and enables you to identify your own critical thinking profile along six dimensions, encapsulated by the acronym CODE ON: cognitive awareness, observation skills, differences, empathy, openness and non-personalisation. There is also a strategy for you to prepare an action plan to improve the areas you wish to focus on. I examine closely three major components of thinking criticially: reasons, assumptions and perspectives. Another important strategy of 're-framing' is presented as a step towards further creativity. There are examples and exercises throughout to help you consolidate your understanding of the concepts and approaches.

After reading this book you can refer back to the sections that best fulfil your needs. I encourage you to think critically about what I say so that you can maintain your quest to think critically while you are learning to think critically.

PART ONE

THE SEVEN KEYS

Overview of the Seven Keys of thinking critically

Minds are like parachutes, they work best when open.
—Lord Thomas Dewar

Imagine you live in the middle of the last millennium. What do you think it would have been like? The Internet doesn't exist, and there are no phones, television, aeroplanes or cars. Sailors fear taking their ships too far lest they fall off the edge of the Earth. Now imagine you live in the future. What would that be like?

People in the western world today don't have the same fears that existed last century about the unknown. If things continue the way they have been I am certain that our understanding of who we are and where we are will be transformed significantly during this coming century. There are many opportunities or new discoveries and new points of view because Nature consists of a multitude of conditions that interact in a multitude of ways.

Think about the universe—the Big Bang, black holes, exploding supernova and other marvels indicate that conditions in the universe are so extreme that we will be rediscovering the nature of reality for a while. It is even plausible for people to talk about the existence not of one single universe but of multiple parallel universes, creating even more possibilities. The universe is an apt metaphor for the seven keys of thinking critically. It is a very sophisticated system, quite contrary to its appearance. We cannot understand our universe with mathematics alone. Like the universe, we cannot understand thinking critically from a single perspective.

The spinning hourglass model

Think about a spinning hourglass model consisting of a hub in the centre and two swirls. The hub attracts, repels and consolidates the two swirls, spinning extremes. The hub represents a group of people open to exploration—it is the essence of our identity and where thinking critically occurs. This is one key and through it we come to know who we are through each other. Ultimately, thinking critically centres upon our interaction, mutual attraction and accountability in an open group.

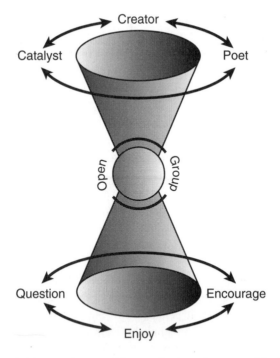

The two spinning ends or swirls attached to the central hub represent the other six keys. One swirl represents three key behaviours that lead to enhancing an individual's skill in thinking critically. This section includes the capacity to *enjoy* thinking critically for itself, the ability to ask basic *questions* and the disposition to *encourage* others to lead them into the rewarding activity of thinking critically. The other swirl represents three roles performed by both individuals and groups that enhance thinking critically at all levels in relation to external environments. The roles are that of becoming a *catalyst* for change by sharing leadership—for example, becoming a *poet* by refining your capacity to use available devices as well as inventing new devices to create difference, and becoming a *creator* with the capacity to break away from existing rules and patterns and inventing new ones. All these six roles represent the creativity swirl of thinking critically.

The three skills surrounding one swirl are egocentric ones that focus on individuals increasing their own awareness of their thinking through introspection. This is done by deliberately enjoying the activity of using our mind for its own sake. There is no need to wait until a problem surfaces before we start to think critically. Asking basic questions is the way to start thinking critically because in essence basic questions unravel fundamental truths that we either take for granted or are unclear about. Only after we have learned to enjoy the process and achieved some mastery are we in a position to encourage others to do the same. Encouraging others is part of the egocentric process of refining our basic skills. The differences that exist between individual people seem to be infinite as are the differences in the universe. Imagine if we could experience the vast differences of the universe! Who would we be and what would we understand?

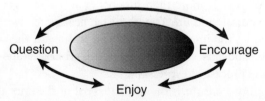

At the hub of the spinning hourglass model is an open group, the basic social unit for thinking critically. Thinking critically in groups and in teams needs to be a major focus of our whole thinking critically effort because this is the testing ground for respect among the members, when they choose to seriously consider each other's point of view. Synergy or wholeness is the ultimate objective of a group on the path of thinking critically. Synergy represents a group energy that is greater than the sum of the contribution of its individual members. It emerges from the respect of each different point of view. It may seem ironic that synergy results, in part, from valuing openness and difference. A team achieves unity when it is free of negative forms of group dynamic such as defensiveness, jealousy, domination and hatred. Members in the group need a mindset of accepting challenge as a healthy, inviting and productive way to interrelate. Being friends and colleagues in adversity—that is, being open to different points of view—is the focus of thinking critically in groups.

   The three key roles surrounding the other swirl are outwardly focused on enlightened self-interest. The role of being a catalyst involves the special skill of being supportive of others, sharing leadership, so that they undergo a change and achieve an effective level of self-sufficiency. Being a catalyst is a leadership role that includes empowering others, freeing them to make the decisions and share the mutual responsibility required to succeed. A catalyst needs a unique quality that the author Michael Gelb calls *sfumato* (all smoked out), a high tolerance for ambiguity and uncertainty. The role of poet is more than just being an encourager. It means inspiring yourself and others with difference. It involves spirit and defiance to let the imagination run wild to suggest the absurd as a possibility. A poet uses the existing tools of art and creates new tools through the process of expression.
   Becoming a creator is the ultimate goal of the critical thinker.
   A goal is simply what we can imagine with the deadline we attach to it. Our external environment is staring at us in the face, daring us to observe what we take for granted with new eyes.

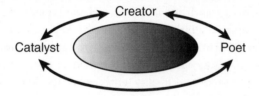

In particular, each individual's own environment within, what is in our heart and mind, is the closest environment yet the most difficult terrain to access. We need to first direct our own thinking critically to see inwardly any blind spots, egocentric myopia, hypocrisy or absurdities. Creativity emerges from the challenge of basic assumptions, from melding unlikely things, from upsetting the balance and the existing patterns and inventing new guidelines, new ways of doing things we take for granted. Discover the unknown in yourself and in your surroundings! Invent new ways of seeing and doing!

The swirl of thinking critically

The astronomer, Edwin Hubble, was the first to demonstrate that the universe is expanding. Our capacity to fathom and appreciate perspectives has also been expanding. For example, presently, galaxies are the largest known structures in the universe. But are there still larger patterns that we have failed to see because we have not yet looked far enough into space? We have not yet been able to observe a parallel universe. We are still searching for a larger-scale pattern that may provide profound insights for theories about the origin of structure in the universe. We are at a similar level of comprehension to this as far as our interpersonal relationships are concerned. Thinking critically allows us to free up our sense of adventure and expand our intimacy through greater knowledge and appreciation of each other.

Why a *spinning* hourglass? Movement is the basis for thinking critically. Openness is only possible if we shift from a singular thought. Perspectives exist at each of the minutest angles from the original thought. Each of the seven keys can be used alone or in combination with any others. Each key can be interpreted in untold ways. Movement exists between the keys through the spinning and the movement up and down the hourglass. This causes the perspectives to shift in relation to each of the keys presented in this book. We have the imaginative capacity to appreciate these moving perspectives simultaneously. The movement is a sign that we are alive and so, thinking critically enables us to demonstrate the unique life within us.

Enjoy thinking critically

Thinking requires leisure time.
—Aristotle, Greek philosopher

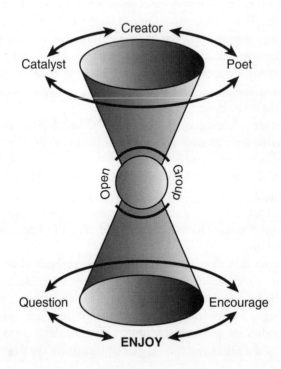

When you spin the hourglass it is a reminder that you should be enjoying thinking in new ways while you are thinking critically. All the keys should be enjoyed in tandem as you start to master them. Here are three things to remember:

1. Thinking critically is a skill that can be learned by anyone. It's not an in-built part of an evolutionary reasoning ability.
2. Thinking critically is learned best when you are feeling relaxed and can enjoy the experience.
3. Thinking critically can be used to make discoveries and solve problems, but try not to focus too hard on the end result. Enjoy thinking critically for itself—don't worry about the solution.

Develop positive self-talk

Thinking makes us the very essence of what we are! The French philosopher, René Descartes' famous saying, 'I think, therefore I am', means that the essence of being human is our capacity to think. When you think you 'talk' to yourself. The talking can be done in words, images or in feelings. Thinking as self-talk means mulling over meanings and feelings within our own minds and bodies. This is the nature of being human.

Descartes is known as the father of the mind–body issue. His main treatise on thinking was first published in 1641, the year before Galileo Galilei died and Isaac Newton was born. He lived at a time when traditional ideas were being questioned and he was smart enough not to publish his book after he heard that Galileo had been condemned by the Inquisition in 1633 for defending the Copernican system, which basically held that the Earth revolved around the sun.

Descartes said that human beings are a synthesis of two kinds of element, mind and body. The mind is conscious, thinks, understands, chooses, senses and imagines. The body has structure, matter, shape, length, height and breadth. Minds are indivisible, whereas bodies are endlessly divisible. The 'I' of the 'I think, therefore I am' is the mind and can, in principle, survive the death of the body. We are born as a bundle of survival reflexes unable to think consciously and to remember very much but gain skills as we grow and develop. When we are asleep we are not aware of our thinking but we still exist. We could not say the opposite of Descartes' statement to be true: I don't think therefore I am not. In spite of these different natures, Descartes thought that mind and body have a causal relationship. The mind causes movement in the body. The brain produces sensation and emotion. This problem of whether the mind is different in nature from the body continues to be a focus of many philosophers and psychologists.

Descartes is one of the most important and influential thinkers in human history and is sometimes called the founder of modern philosophy. His thinking in part has persuaded scientists over the centuries to adopt a clockwork mechanics model for life processes. Today, we have discarded a number of things Descartes told us. Far from being a single entity, each person's consciousness seems to be built up from a number of mini-consciousnesses at different levels. Some scientists today have shown that we see colour, form and motion in that order, mini- or nanoseconds apart and that these separate conscious events could very well synthesise to produce the overall consciousness we experience.

Nevertheless, we can use Descartes' statement to think about 'self-talk', the silent dialogue we engage in with ourselves as we go about our daily activities. Think about your own self-talk. Does it reflect your own sense of self-esteem and worth? The fact is that self-talk is incredibly powerful. We are who we *think* we are. If we think poorly about ourselves, it's likely that we behave in a negative way.

A good place to begin with thinking critically is to develop positive self-talk. When we are relaxed and happy, satisfied with our job and interpersonal relationships we have an ideal state to play with ideas and explore notions and absurdities that would not appeal to us in situations of stress and unhappiness. We should delight at the mental feats we can perform with our whole body. What I am stressing here is that we think with our whole body, not just with our minds. Thinking critically should be an enjoyable experience.

Try saying to yourself, 'I *think* I'm great, therefore I *am* great!'
How does it feel? Try other statements, using your own words to fill
in the blanks: 'I think I'm _____, therefore I am _____'.

Try these:

- I think I'm incompetent, therefore I am incompetent.
- I think I'm smart, therefore I am smart.
- I think I'm busy, therefore I am busy.

Let's take this a step further. Our mindset can lead us to behave the
way we believe we are. Catch yourself thinking this way and over-
ride your mindset to see what might happen. Try and welcome the
experience of having some intellectual fun. Change the parameters:

- I think I'm busy therefore I will take a stroll in the garden and
  take time to smell the roses.
- I think I have strong feelings therefore I will go south (some-
  times) when I feel like going north.
- I think I'm a critical thinker, therefore I am an individual.
  I am what I choose to think that I am.

Develop the capacity to reflect

The Greek philosopher, Socrates, said, 'the unexamined life is not
worth living'. In other words, life becomes unrewarding and meaningless if we don't develop the capacity for self-reflection. It is a
reminder that we should not become a society of non-thinkers.
Rather, we should seek to understand the complexities of our existence and try to live according to what we decide we value.

Socrates also said, 'Know yourself'. To know yourself it's
necessary to know others and to understand your environments.
The greater the diversity of experience you are able to encompass,
the more likely it is that your appreciation and understanding of
yourself and others will grow.

When I introduce my students to the idea of thinking about
their thinking they become quite fascinated. A number of them

wonder why they haven't thought about their thinking before. Why is it that so many people do not appear to be aware of the role of reflection in the way your life turns out? When we haven't reflected about our thinking we haven't really known how we think and how it works. Non-reflective thinkers do not notice that they are perceiving something from a particular perspective, that they are stating conclusions through drawing inferences and making deductions. They are not sharply aware that they are always making assumptions. There is a saying, 'Don't assume, it makes an *ass* of *u* and *me*'. The point is that thinking could not occur without assumptions. I think therefore I assume.

The very act of assuming is the thinking process itself! We all naturally reason about what is valuable to ourselves and to others. Some of us may be sceptical that reasoning can be useful because we think that values depend mainly on our feelings and emotions and that feelings and emotions are not really controlled by our reasoning and knowledge. It's common to hear people say: 'That doesn't feel right to me; what is important is how you feel about the situation; if you don't feel like it then don't do it'. Just because we all make these sort of assumptions doesn't mean that we have not reasoned and used our knowledge alongside our emotion. You can't really separate the thoughts, knowledge and experience of the mind and those of the body! Feeling is a particular way of thinking. It is thinking without the relevant ideas. Let me illustrate this point.

Sarah was holidaying with friends in Barcelona and they were visiting the great cathedral of La Sacra Famiglia. As they were about to wind their way down the steep steps of the spire, Thomas, whom she disliked, reached out, causing her to fall and injure herself. When Thomas protested that he was simply trying to help her down the steps she had an opportunity to change her feelings because of what she now knew. Knowledge makes a difference to our feelings and is often a precursor to them.

In another sense feelings and thoughts are inextricably bound but the awareness is not always obvious. For example, the thought of home conjures up particular feelings. When you think of friends and foes then different feelings come to you. Think of a storm—can you imagine the range of feelings this thought will spontaneously conjure up in people! Emotion multiplies the power of the thinking and drives it further.

Another reason some of us are sceptical about the power thinking has on our values is because we believe we are relativists—that is, there is no single truth or reality. Some will mistakenly believe that one person's values are unrelated to another person's. There is no such thing as objective truth because one person's judgement is as good as anyone else's but if you are powerful and rich then your judgement is valued more. In this case value judgements are seen as opinions that are not necessarily based on facts or on respect of other's opinions. For example, which of these statements do you agree with?

> Al Qaeda are terrorists.
> Al Qaeda are freedom fighters.
> Palestinians are terrorists.
> Palestinians are freedom seekers.

It is easy to be cynical about the value of thinking critically if we believe that it is impossible to agree and arrive at mutually shared conclusions. Of course, this is difficult in a complex world but not impossible, even though it may not always be desirable, especially during creativity.

A capacity for reflection involves awareness and control of one's emotions. Feelings and emotions need to act on the thinking once the thinking is established. When emotion is not separated from the thought then the emotion tends to dictate the decisions. Edward de Bono reminds us that 'without thinking, feeling is tyranny'. Feelings establish priorities, present direction, provide pressure, dictate obligation but these work best within the confines of prior thinking. It's the ideas that channel the emotions but then the emotions power-up the ideas even further. Emotions are the aesthetics and beauty of life as well as the possible horrors, but progress occurs when we harness them. Reflection gives us that power to harness our emotions.

If we do not think about our thinking it is highly likely that problems will occur in our lives because of it. We will not understand the importance of criteria to judge the value of our beliefs, to judge the soundness of our judgements, to assess if our thinking is faulty and to know which type of thinking might be best suited to producing what we desire. We put ourselves in great danger of unwittingly deceiving ourselves and others. We might continue to create and maintain favourable illusions, feel that our beliefs are reasonable, perhaps beyond reproach and maintain a false and full sense of confidence in ourselves without acknowledging uncertainty. We would not question our own thinking but be happily dominated by our own personal tendencies and prejudices, refusing to be open to other points of view.

When we delight in the pursuit of excellence in thinking we will not be defensive about being self-correcting, about being open to ideas contrary to our own, about valuing differences, about the importance of sharpening our perceptual capacity and about respecting the thinking and views of others. We will respect that thinking and feeling—that is, the whole mind and whole body—operate together to make us what we are. We will acknowledge that feeling is the engine for thinking; when the engine overheats thinking will stop, when the engine runs within its tolerance levels thinking performance will be at its best.

You will develop your capacity to reflect when you take time to think critically. To do this you will need to practise new skills, the keys to thinking critically, and monitor your progress, perhaps using the Critical Reflection Inventory (CRI) or other tools available in this book. It will be useful to ask your colleagues or friends to observe your behaviour and your communication interchanges to notice if your capacity to reflect is changing. This capacity to reflect should increase when you raise your mental awareness, when you try to observe more carefully, when you are open to points of view different from your own and actively seek out those different perspectives. Your capacity to reflect increases if you especially try to take notice of your feelings and try to channel them into your thoughts to improve your habits.

Develop creativity

The secret of thinking creatively about problems is to focus your energy and your concentration. If you can do this without worrying,

observing what is around you, you will discover what is important
to you. Keep the issues in your mind and try to relish a sense of
exploration. Solutions may come as a result of your reflections,
sometimes when you least expect it.

Solutions to problems may also come from unexpected directions. For example, in 1928, Scottish bacteriologist Sir Alexander
Fleming discovered penicillin by some quite surprising coincidences.
Fleming's focus was on experimenting but of course he also wanted
to make a discovery. When some mucus accidentally dripped from
his nose onto his petri dish it eventually became the first anti-
bacteria substance or 'antibiotic'. Seven years later a straying spore
blew in through the window where he was experimenting with the
same solution and landed on his dish. This led to the creation of
penicillin, an antibiotic that is now used to great effect to kill infectious germs, including those that cause diphtheria and pneumonia.
Fleming's work owed much to the discoveries of Louis Pasteur, the
French scientist who invented the process of pasteurisation, which
kills harmful bacteria in foods. Pasteur believed that 'fortune
favours the prepared mind'. In other words, keeping your brain
sharp by thinking critically will produce benefits.

The classic exclamation in response to a welcome discovery was
said by Archimedes, a Greek mathematician and inventor. He
was called on by King Hiero to analyse a gift, a supposedly solid
gold crown he had received as a tribute from a conquered enemy.
Suspecting it had other, inferior metals in it, Hiero asked Archimedes
to identify how much gold was in the crown in order to give him
some idea of how much his enemy thought he was worth. At the
time no one knew how to measure the different densities of mixed
metals.

Archimedes reflected long and hard but the answer didn't come
immediately. He didn't worry about it, but let the problem swirl
around in his head. One day as he got into a bath full of water, a
flash of inspiration came to him. As he lowered himself into the tub,
he noticed that some of the water began to spill over the sides of the
tub. What was happening, he realised, was that his body mass was
displacing an equal amount of liquid. All he had to do was to put
the crown in a full basin of water and measure how much water

flowed over the edge of the basin. From the amount of water displaced he could then work out how much gold was in the crown. All he needed to do was to compare this result to the water displaced by a similar sized object made of solid gold. Archimedes had discovered the principle of specific gravity. He jumped for joy out of the bathtub, hardly remembering that he was naked, and ran through the streets of Syracuse shouting, '*Eureka!*', meaning, 'I've found it!'

So, what produces creativity? What matters with discovery is that you are 'intent' on discovery, that you are searching for something and that you can maintain a focus. The trick is to try and not worry about the solution—enjoy the journey. To focus on the data available, to observe what you can and to keep the issues in your mind and to enjoy the exploration are the key things. The solutions will come if they are meant to, probably when you least expect it. Einstein's greatest discovery, the theory of relativity, came not from new experiments but from a mind shift, a change in paradigm. He was able to interpret in a stunningly new way data previously collected and interpreted by other scientists.

Another example is the 'Superstring theory', which disputes that matter is made up of tiny particles. Instead, the theory observes the data (matter) and interprets it in a stunningly new way: matter consists of vibrating patterns that resonate at various frequencies thus manifesting themselves as particles in matter—just as the different vibrating patterns of a cello's string produce distinct musical notes. So we no longer have the particles but the music of the universe.

Creativity involves thinking obliquely, observing laterally the information that has been available to everyone else's observation but that no one else has been able to interpret with a fresh perspective. Creativity comes through continual use of the skill of changing our recognition patterns to shake us out of our logic and cultural pressures to observe in accepted ways. All the inventors of the modern age have made their discoveries through a mind shift by being open to ideas and by succeeding in perceiving things differently.

Exercises

Thoughts create action

Have some fun by filling in the following statements and in the process discover some of your mindsets and attitudes. The thought— I *think*—in the first half of the statement carries over into the action—*I am*—in the second half. For example, 'I think I am at peace, therefore I am at peace'. 'I think I am offended, therefore I am offended'. You can change the thought if you want to. You can choose to accept the opinions of other people or you can create your own thoughts. After you fill in the following statements, go back and assess if they are thoughts you want to own or if you have taken on the thoughts of others.

I think _____ therefore I am _____
I think _____ therefore I am _____
I think _____ therefore I am _____

Don't worry about the solution—enjoy thinking for itself.

Take time to reflect on yourself

Think about your own history of thinking by filling in the blanks below.

The very first thought I ever had was:

_____

The very first thing I ever really believed in was:

_____

The first things my parents wanted me to think about were:

_____
_____
_____

The best teacher I ever had encouraged me to think (describe *how*, e.g. 'carefully'):

_____

The best friend I ever had encouraged me to think (describe *how*, e.g. 'quickly'):

_____

The best employer I ever had encouraged me to think (describe *how*, e.g. 'like her'):

_____

My favourite thoughts are:

_____
_____
_____

Important insights I have had in the past are:

_____
_____
_____

Key 2

Start with basic questions

When I told my mum that my results consisted of five Fs and one D she asked me if I was spending too much time on one subject.
—Francesco Sofo

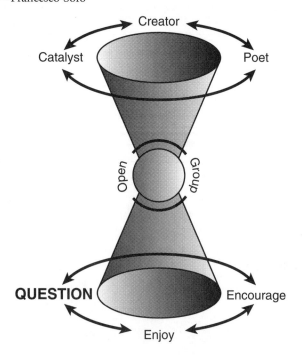

When you spin the hourglass it is a reminder that you should be much more aware that you are using questions purposefully to think critically. All the keys should have questioning as one of the ingredients. As you go around the merry-go-round of the spinning hourglass you should be feeling the power of your questions gently breeze through your mind.

Basic questions lead to thinking critically because they question the most fundamental level of knowledge structure. However, sometimes people simply don't ask basic questions. Why? Because they believe it might make them look foolish. In other words, they prefer to remain in a state of ignorance than risk exposing their own ignorance. Here's an example of a famous disaster that happened because some people omitted to ask basic—and, as it turned out, crucial—questions.

This story was told by the late Reg Revans, the inventor of a new business approach called Action Learning. His father was an investigator for the British government. The *Titanic*, the luxury ship that was built to be unsinkable, actually sank on its maiden voyage on 14 April 1912. Over 1400 passengers died. How could this have happened? Surely the professionals involved in the building of such a magnificent vessel should have been able to prevent a catastrophe? A report produced by the British government revealed that some of those involved in the project had indeed been concerned. They did have serious questions about the ship's safety but admitted that they did not ask them. Why? Because no one else had raised the issue. Perhaps they might have felt some professional foolishness in asking what they termed the 'dumb' questions.

So-called 'dumb' questions are really basic questions of fact and description. What is it? What does it do? And, if you're in the business of making money, what does it cost?

Value analysis

> My boss, I talk to him five or six times a year. But the guy in
> the business unit, I talk to him every day.
> —Tom Anthony, General Electric's leading inventor

The US company General Electric (GE) dominated industrial research through the first half of the twentieth century and re-invented itself several times in the latter half establishing engineering standards and driving the boundaries of solid-state physics, nuclear attention and astronomy, winning Nobel prizes. In a five-year period after World War II GE spent US$2 million to develop value analysis techniques. At the end of the twentieth century GE sales surpassed $US100 billion annually with a scientific staff of over 1100 and a research budget of about $200 million annually. GE, the world's top patent holder, has delivered value world-wide with better industrial diamonds and other super-hard materials, remote monitoring systems that track aircraft engines in flight, the reinforced plastic fan blades for the super-quiet and efficient Boeing 777 aircraft and computed tomography scanners that cut imaging timing from minutes to seconds—for example, trans-forming MRI data into accurate 3-D images instantaneously.

Tom Anthony, GE's top researcher, has had granted, on aver-age, seven patents each year over a 30-year period. He jokes that his secret to success is good lawyers and an ardent uninterrupted focus on the problem until he solves it. He compares his passion for inventions with his passion for bee-keeping, both requiring quick-paced but careful work, not upsetting the status quo (queen bee and honey production) and keeping safe during intense periods of super-concentration that cause you to obliterate the rest of life. He is responsible for the ultra-fast production methods for microchips and manufacturing methods of super-hard materials.

The idea of value analysis came from David Erlicher, vice-president of purchasing for GE. During World War II he was seconded to the US Department of Defense to assist with procure-ment. Many items were scarce during the war and he often received requisitions he could not satisfy. What he did was to ask the person making the requisition to analyse the functions of the item and find cheaper alternatives of acceptable quality. After the war he recom-mended this method of purchasing to Harry Winnie, vice-president of engineering, who agreed to try it on two provisos: that there should be no reduction in reliability or saleability (in other words, the team must not recommend cheap, unreliable substitutes but rather, simpler, more reliable and less costly ones) and second, that no person should be asked to defend an earlier decision. From this, the development of value analysis has continued to the present day.

A key focus of value analysis involves asking basic questions and then developing alternatives. Essentially, it is a disciplined thinking system designed to achieve the best value for money. Through such careful analysis many appliances at GE were improved. Take, for example, the humble toaster. The number of movable parts were greatly reduced, which had a profitable impact because it reduced production costs, maintenance costs and improved reliability. Sales increased because of reliability and improved functions—for example, automatic pop-up.

Another example of how using value analysis can save money is a company that overhauled water meters. They wanted to build a new factory to expand its operations. The problem was that all procurement funds for the financial year had been spent. Although maintenance funds were available, middle management had a policy of not using maintenance funds for procurement. What to do? Value analysis went back to the basic questions:

- How much does it cost to overhaul an old water meter?—$50.
- How much would it cost to buy a new water meter?—$40.

From the answers to these questions, it was obvious that it was cheaper to buy new meters. Senior management decided to do away with the restrictive policy of withholding the maintenance funds and used the money in the maintenance fund to buy new meters. The old ones were sold as scrap, netting the company $500 000. As well, the company had saved itself the cost of a new building.

Function analysis is the creative method used to determine the value of something—it is the tool of value analysis. Function analysis, which is used extensively and successfully by businesses around the world, is a creative problem-solving technique. The function analysis technique addresses the basic questions of:

- What is it?
- What does it do?

- What else does it do?
- What must it do?
- What does it cost?
- What alternative methods can be used to achieve the same functions?
- What do the alternatives cost?

After asking these basic questions and considering the answers, a higher order question is then asked. A higher order question is one that requires us to make a judgement about value and acceptability, such as, are the alternatives acceptable in terms of aesthetics, quality, performance criteria, life cycle costs etc.

Here's an example of how function analysis can work to save costs. A prison needed to be upgraded to accommodate a hundred more inmates. It was decided that the recreation area—the quadrangle—should be surrounded by an inner security fence. This would cost $100 000—a lot of money. Function analysis was put to work.

What was the fence for? Initially, the answer was that its function was to provide a barrier and prevent escape, just as the security fence around the perimeter of the complex already did. Then it was suggested that this inner fence didn't actually need to prevent escape—the perimeter fence did this—but to delineate the recreation space, provide a boundary and indicate a 'sterile area', a 'no-go zone'.

What would it cost to delineate the space? A standard fence would cost $10 000. It would reliably perform the function at a fraction of the cost. An even cheaper option was suggested by a senior security expert. A thick white line would adequately perform the function. The cost? $1000.

A key assumption of function analysis is that everything has a function and that function is at the very heart of analysis. Value is tied to cost and all cost is tied to function. In business, customers want functions.

There are two chief types of function: 'use' and 'aesthetic'. Customers get maximum value when use functions are achieved at the lowest costs. For example, when someone buys a chair they buy the use function that a chair has to offer—that is, support and comfort. The aesthetic function is an 'add-on'. If the chair has been designed by a famous furniture maker, it might give the customer pleasure to look at it as well as to sit on it, so it's also providing an aesthetic function.

Many systems require both use and aesthetic functions. A good example is the Sydney Opera House. A major part of the cost of building this structure was to achieve aesthetic function. And this function achieved valuable returns: its unique aesthetics attract millions of dollars in tourism annually. In fact, the Opera House has become an icon for Australia.

There's no magic in thinking critically although it may seem so when you achieve a great result like one of the examples above.

Four stages of thinking critically

Obtaining fresh insights is wonderful but it can be a long process. It takes time for new ideas to be born and to mature. Thinking critically is not generally a process that brings immediate solutions. What usually happens is that in asking questions about facts and information that we know, we educate ourselves and come to learn about different aspects and more details of the particular problem we're facing. The best thing is to 'incubate' the new information we've gained and just let it sit in our mind and sink into our being. Eventually, the thoughts themselves may reveal a useful solution. Thus, the process of thinking critically can be divided into four stages: agitate, educate, incubate and innovate.

1. Agitate: ask basic questions and challenge the hidden assumptions.
2. Educate: find out as much as possible about the issues.
3. Incubate: let all the knowledge settle and ferment; wait for the wine; allow intuition to work.
4. Innovate: allow the ideas to flow when they are ready; try the new ideas.

Remember: once you start the process the steps become enmeshed and circular.

Many modern inventors and Nobel prize winners use this method. They start with the basic questions: What must it do? They educate themselves on the basics and ensure they know all there is to know about their interest—for example, who else has tried this and why did they fail? Then they let it brew and allow intuition to play its part. For some, intuition comes through stumbling on one piece at a time. For example, Paul MacCready won the Henry Kramer Prize in 1977 for his aircraft, which made the first sustained controlled flight powered solely by the pilot's muscles. He did it with an aircraft that was 'heavier-than-air'. Since then Paul's company, Gossamer Condor, has pioneered ecologically sound vehicles for land, sea and air that use alternative power sources. Paul loves to work on about a dozen projects simultaneously as one helps the other. His intuitions work on one idea at a time. For example, while reading a magazine he will stumble on a piece of the jigsaw and then while waiting at an airport another piece will fall into place. He turns from one context to another and finds that the random ideas produce solutions.

The enigmatic challenge of circularity

> 'Don't let us quarrel,' the White Queen said in an anxious tone. 'What is the cause of lightning?'
> 'The cause of lightning,' Alice said very decidedly, for she felt quite certain about this, 'is thunder—no, no!' she hastily corrected herself. 'I meant the other way.'
> 'It's too late to correct it,' said the Red Queen: 'when you've once said a thing, that fixes it, and you must take the consequences.'
> —Lewis Carroll, *Through the Looking Glass*

Sometimes asking basic questions might seem like a waste of time—we already know that, so why ask it again? The truth is, when we are stuck and looking for ideas we tend to repeat the same ideas and questions in our head. It is helpful to adopt a new approach to what might seem a useless type of circularity by asking the same questions and having the same thoughts. Circularity, rather than staying in a rut, will get us out of a rut.

Human behaviour can be seen as circular—people's actions are both a cause and a result and can be sources of problems and consequences. Using the idea of circularity can allow us to see with new eyes. Any statement contains within it an infinite number of questions and assumptions. A circular view of reality challenges us to identify the most relevant and useful aspects among the different views we could see.

Recursion (circularity) is a dominant and powerful phenomenon that is pervasive in our universe. Recursion is where structures continually fold in upon themselves. One example is the mythical snake Ouroborous that continuously eats its own tail. The snake is a symbol of patterns repeating themselves, just as we tend to repeat our thoughts and our behaviours.

Repetition is not necessarily a bad thing. If all repetition in the universe was eliminated we would end up with a very frugal situation, probably no situation! This is because the simplest of objects, such as an atom, cannot exist without having a repetition of its subatomic components. Thinking critically allows us to recognise and appreciate circularity in order to notice simplicity within complexity.

The ordering of streams of actions is more important than single actions. All actions are part of some organised interaction. Seeing a relationship between things requires 'double description', the ability to see different orders of pattern. Double description allows us to perceive behaviour at a higher logical level. Just as two eyes can see a third (depth) dimension, two descriptions can uncover patterns and relationships. The two types of description can be classified as complementary or symmetrical.

Before a classification of an action or event can be made, a decision must be made on how an action is related to the preceding action and to the subsequent action. A symmetrical relationship results in a replication, where one action stimulates and is stimulated by a similar action. A complementary relationship is where one action is preceded and followed by different actions. Both types can represent a kind of dance, where professional practice, conversations, family dinners and international conflicts are organised according to their own rules of dance.

A doctor's basic act of knowing and understanding what is happening with a patient is made through the creation of a difference. When the doctor distinguishes one pattern from another he develops knowledge of the patient. The distinctions—for example, between symptom and intervention, problem and solution—enable the doctor to work in a discerning way. Making distinctions is the starting point for any description, analysis, decision or action. For the doctor, a particular meaning comes into existence when an event is taken apart and rebuilt and when boundaries are discerned where it is judged best. In this way the doctor together with the patient can co-create an infinite number of scenarios through making and re-making distinctions. Some hypotheses are created until the doctor makes a final judgement and a diagnosis with reference to the 'whole' person.

Consider the act of the doctor picking up a pen and writing a prescription for the patient. An analytical way of understanding this event is to see all the separate entities: the doctor, the pen, the prescription and the patient. The doctor acts on the pen to produce a prescription and this is given to the patient. Thinking critically is a different analytical framework that starts with the whole rather than with the parts. If we view the scenario of the doctor, the pen and the prescription as a product of our making distinctions then we exercise our freedom to order the sequence of events in any way we choose. We might like to argue that prescriptions cause doctors to write them or that patients cause prescriptions to cause doctors to write them. The point is that we can discern the world in an infinite number of ways depending on the distinctions we choose to make. In observing the doctor writing the script we can create a different pattern of organisation. We can see the prescription causing the pen to move to the doctor's hand as logical as the acceptable sequencing of events where the doctor picks up the pen and writes the script.

The traditional view is that the doctor treats the patient through a given intervention such as a prescription. What if a doctor were to imagine a patient's behaviour as an intervention that provokes the doctor to come up with a useful solution. Treatment is successful when the patient provokes the doctor to say or prescribe the appropriate action. In this reverse view the doctor's behaviours are problematic when they fail to help the patient. But take note, both the traditional and alternative points of view are incomplete because both are linear. It is the recursive action between the two scenarios among others that leads to a solution.

If we remember that thinking critically means that we take on a wholistic perspective, that we always keep the whole picture in mind, then in this case we will highlight the patient and doctor as part of a whole picture in a dialectical relationship embedded within other pictures. This aspect of thinking critically encourages us to focus on a circular or recursive view of events. This perspective means that patients treat doctors at the same time doctors treat patients. It means we can view behaviour as connected circularly, which means that any behaviour or event is simultaneously a source of problems and a consequence or a prescription within that scenario.

Using circularity is like a pool of water catching a pebble with its embrace of circular wave-like ripples converging on the point of contact. Circular thinking helps us to make precise distinctions that allow a unique and useful interpretation of experience. The passionate questions generate answers just like fine distinctions generate useful descriptions and further questions.

The doctor's questions, distinctions, hypotheses and descriptions help generate the context of the problem at hand. Doctors and patients cooperate in constructing a shared reality through the distinctions they co-create. This co-creation of reality can be enhanced through the use of teams—for example, involving doctors behind mirrors as participants in the consultation process. Co-consultation is another option. Describing who the doctor and patient are always prescribes a way of intervening. In many cases this is taken for granted.

My suggestion is to identify and learn to move with the patterns and then break the patterns. Create difference. Thinking critically is about difference. Break your patterns and rebuild them. Break your habits and rebuild them. Yes, I've said that twice! When you have found a technique that works, think of how to change it. My advice is, don't take my advice. If you agree to take this advice, you won't and if you don't take this advice, you will.

Thinking critically is designed to upset our balance of thoughts, to help us overcome assumptions that prevent us from achieving our desires. Although some insights may not be exactly what we expected, they should not be upsetting in themselves. Sometimes the insights stubbornly remain hidden despite our best efforts. If this happens, it's worth holding on to the pleasure of your capacity to engage in a questioning process that is constructively sceptical. Exploring, challenging and trying to think of alternatives are pleasurable activities in themselves.

Exercises

Analysing function

Analyse the items on the list below by asking basic questions to gauge their value and functions and then look for alternatives that can perform the same functions. I have done the first one for you.

Decide which of the four items above give you value for money by asking basic questions. For example, do shopping lists need to be written in ink? Is it inconvenient to have to fill a pen with ink? Do I need to show anyone that I have enough money to own a fountain pen? Will a biro do just as well and is it much cheaper? Is the aesthetic function important? Am I prepared to spend money on a fountain pen?

It helps to complete this exercise with a colleague. Asking basic questions works best with an attitude of being helpful and sharing. Questions should be asked in a helpful, supportive and unpresumptive way and as a result, there should be no feelings of embarrassment or stupidity. Remember that asking questions is an opportunity to explore the situation, not necessarily to arrive at a solution. Exploration is critical to the process because it helps to defuse any defensiveness, to uncover new connections, to understand at a deeper level and to seek delight in the journey.

Reflect on a project

Think of a recent project you completed successfully. Maybe you redesigned your garden or created a garden from scratch, or you

Fountain Pen	What does it do?	Makes marks; signifies status; indicates wealth of user etc.
	How much does it cost?	$5–$2000
	What else can perform these functions? How much do they cost?	Pencil 60 cents Biro $1.50–$5
Chair	What does it do?	
	How much does it cost?	
	What else can perform these functions? How much do they cost?	
House	What does it do?	
	How much does it cost?	
	What else can perform these functions? How much do they cost?	
Book	What does it do?	
	How much does it cost?	
	What else can perform these functions? How much do they cost?	

bought a home or renovated your existing home. Now, imagine you are re-living that experience and ask yourself some basic questions about the project. You can create your own. Remember that a basic question tries to elicit facts and descriptions. Examples of basic questions are: How big is it? What colour is it? Where is it exactly? How much does it cost? How long does it take? Where do you purchase materials? Who will help? These are not questions of opinion.

Anyone could ask these questions and you would expect the answer to be the same or close approximations. A sample would be:

1. A project I completed successfully recently was: _____
2. These are the things I wanted to achieve: _____
3. These were the core requirements to complete the project:

_____

Now think of a project you want to do and address these basic questions and others that are important to you.

1. What would I like to achieve in carrying out this project? _____
2. What are the core requirements? _____
3. What must I do now? _____
4. What must I do in the long term? _____
5. What must be different when I finish this project? _____

Things I must do now	Things I must do in the longer term

When you become more systematic about the projects you under-take it is likely that you will achieve insights you did not expect.

Become an encourager

No person has the right to dictate what other people should perceive, create or produce, but all should be encouraged to reveal themselves, their perceptions and emotions, and to build confidence in the creative spirit.

—Ansel Adams, photographer

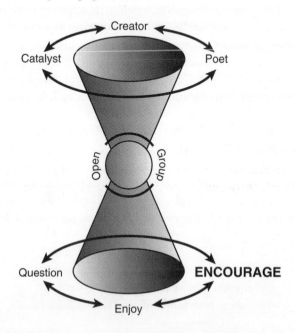

When you spin the hourglass it is a reminder that you are travelling through the same space as others who are on the path of improvement. It is an opportunity to share your enthusiasm, to inspire and encourage those you interact with daily. All the keys should be a trigger for encouragement as you start to turn them.

Whether you are a CEO, a business or project manager, a supervisor or a worker without management responsibility, you can help your colleagues and learn from them along the way by becoming an encourager. By inspiring other people it is possible to explore your own potential as well as that of other people. A key tool for a prosperous future is cooperative thinking critically.

How will embracing thinking critically benefit you and your business? We are fortunate in Australia to have democracy in the workplace. In theory, we are free to speak our minds and to ask questions. In an ideal work situation our contribution is valued, we are listened to and our views are taken into account. This does not mean that everyone will do what we want but it does mean we can initiate discussion about better ways to do things. We have the right to contribute to decision making.

Managers and bosses in a democratic society have an obligation to listen, to empathise and to take into account the views and contributions of their employees. To do this, they need to be clear about their own vision and to communicate it to others. They need to continually share the vision and their passion for it, and to authorise staff to contribute to the vision and, by necessity, to help re-shape it. Managers have an obligation to create confidence, commitment and competence in all employees to cooperatively achieve common goals.

Individual mastery of thinking critically and team effectiveness are inextricably connected. They are processes that never end because our world and our web of interpersonal relationships are always changing. Encouragement leads to more effective teamwork.

> Those who are lifting the world upward and onward are those
> who encourage more than criticize.
> —Elizabeth Harrison, professor, author, organist

To be an inspiration also encourages others to think differently. Ted Turner—team builder, empire maker, winner of the America's Cup ocean yacht race, environmentalist and donator of $1 billion (a third of his wealth) to the United Nations for peaceful purposes —is an excellent example of someone who inspires. He has demonstrated unusual open-mindedness, tenacity and change when he created the first 24-hour global news channel, Cable Network News (CNN). Many of us took it for granted that we could and perhaps should see the news only once or twice daily— at six or eleven in the evening. This situation was reminiscent of the Dark Ages when only the church hierarchy and politicians had education, sharing only what they wanted and keeping people in the dark. Ted wanted to do news like no one else had ever thought of or done, so creating CNN was an important step in the democratisation of information.

To begin, learn to inspire

You may have already thought that the skill of encouraging is one of leadership and of effective team work. Social and interpersonal relationships are the key elements of leadership and team expertise. Leadership not only designs the purpose of the enterprise, it also means to be of service to the people that follow, which is the paradox of leadership. It's not all one way; leaders have to develop a productive interpersonal adhesion. Leaders relay their personally constructed values, their vision and their gut purpose to the people who are part of their team, a team which they are part of. Leaders also have a natural feeling to serve, to put their people first and to encourage the heart of the team. Great leaders inspire and unify the aspirations of their followers by being of service to them and helping them achieve their common wisdom. Leadership, like a coin, has two sides where each is a necessary and different part of its identity. Effective leaders design and serve as part of their leadership. Without this simple but powerful twin structure of design and service people suffer unnecessarily. Foolish leadership creates suffering of different kinds: financial, spiritual and emotional.

I believe that any person's life will be filled with constant and
unexpected encouragement, if he or she makes up their mind
to do their level best each day, and as nearly as possible reach-
ing the high water mark of pure and useful living.
—Booker T. Washington, educational reformer and author

Douglas Bader is an excellent example of an encourager of
thinking critically. He was shocked and saddened when his aero-
batic plane crashed in 1931 and he had to have both of his legs
amputated. Anyone would have thought that was the end of his
career in the British airforce, but Bader was back in the air force
flying spitfires when World War II broke out. This was a
triumphant demonstration of his determination to overcome his
disability. He insisted on fighting at Dunkirk, which he did so
magnificently, and was then given his own squadron. His courage,
determination, leadership and success were evident to his squadron
from the first day, when he demonstrated his creative tactics and
shot down two German planes.

Bader's method was two pronged: to keep his squadron tightly
grouped and to then focus on disrupting the enemy formations.
Once he created a chink in the enemy formation the opposition's
planes became easy targets. He told the squadron that having
strength in numbers was no real consolation, it was important for
them to identify and deal with the weaknesses of the enemy formations. When some pilots suggested the enemy were smart and
would soon learn to re-form, Bader encouraged them to become
true learning squadrons and to master the art even more quickly
than the enemy. He challenged their basic knowledge and attitude
of the superiority of the enemy planes. He encouraged them to
question their own beliefs about the enemy—were the enemy
smarter than them? He told them they should not let any negative
thoughts deter them just as he did not allow his handicap to
prevent him from overcoming insurmountable odds.

Bader's encouragement had gone a step further than just
sharing his ideas. The discussion and sharing of ideas between the
men and Bader were tremendous encouragements to the squadron
as a whole. They were united in purpose through Bader's leadership

of inspiring them with his vision and encouragement. Bader led a strong formation of 60 fighters against enemy bombers and together with other British formations inflicted heavy losses on the German airforce. Bader's tactics were highly successful as the tightly formed squadrons were able to show their strength and skill by breaking many enemy formations. Unfortunately, Bader was shot down over France a year later and spent the rest of the war in prison. This was not a good ending for a leader! But it was an opportunity for other leaders to emerge to revitalise and to be of service to each other. Once having experienced an encouraging and inspiring approach, the RAF wanted to follow the legacy that Bader left. His tactics were soon adopted throughout the whole RAF. New leaders emerged and reiterated the urging and challenges begun by Bader.

What did they learn from Bader? They learned they could remain committed to the vision; they could challenge their erroneous assumptions that the enemy was smarter and unstoppable; they could design different approaches to problems which each leader could ruminate on individually and within their squadrons by continuing their dialogue. It required a focus of energy and commitment to succeed.

Encouraging and challenging your employees can also lead to potentially higher levels of performance. However, particular structures are necessary to enable this to happen so you may need to change the way your company is currently functioning. Issues to consider include:

- ensure staff can influence decisions and direction
- demonstrate appreciation for the ordinary and extraordinary
- create opportunities to share what is special in the workplace
- take time to acknowledge successes and to celebrate small and big wins
- improve reporting relationships to facilitate mutual accountability
- empower work teams and groups to be energised and focused
- ensure intrinsic reward systems take priority
- use performance indicators to develop people's interests and skills

- refine communication systems and procedures
- align sponsors, mentors and managers to cooperate.

Sharing the vision

A shared vision is possible with a deep level of encouragement. It can promote good relationships between employees and help build corporate identity. It can lead to cooperation to create a strong culture based on agreed values. Identity is important to any business effort because the corporate effort is designed to create that identity. We see it all the time when enterprises articulate their visions: they want to be the premier provider of a particular service; they want to be the employer of choice in their industry; they want to be number one in their perceived strength. The challenge is how do they achieve that vision?

You would think that when you have a strong vision of who and what you want to be that bound to that vision would be a clear pathway from where you are. The truth is such strong visions are rare and the pathways to achieve them are also obscure. If enterprises imitate each other as a pathway they find the effect of such imitation usually leads to mediocrity. Businesses often see their vision as achievable through the re-structuring game, which means mergers and acquisitions. Identity then comes from buying additional growth rather than actually 'growing' it. Cost-cutting is another method, sometimes called 'right-sizing' or 'downsizing'. 'Zero defects' is a catchcry which is an impossible goal to achieve. Once the fat goes, further cutbacks destroy the muscle, the enterprise's power to perform.

Quality focus and customer service are more recent approaches adopted by businesses. Both of these require creativity to produce a unique identity from the vision. Both of these require thinking critically to handle information in new ways, to identify and challenge assumptions and to build knowledge about the vision. Critical and creative thinking should lead the way in handling information about the enterprise and incorporating other methods of knowing the business, such as data analysis, computer simulation, statistical and analytical thinking.

Both critical and creative thinking are required to not only produce the vision but to also know how to share it. These tools are about introducing new perspectives and new ways of proceeding. They are about showing people that following a different path is more viable and sensible than the previous one. Difference makes more sense and is seen as logical in hindsight, once understood and adopted.

Some of you may know the story of Spartacus, a Roman gladiator in the century before Christ's birth. He led a slave uprising against the Roman legions and defeated them twice. Finally, Spartacus and his army of slaves were defeated by General Marcus Crassus after a long siege and battle. Naturally, the general was keen to identify Spartacus among the thousand surviving slaves in order to make an example of him.

He offered to spare the slaves from crucifixion if they turned Spartacus over to him. To spare his comrades, Spartacus stood up and declared, 'I am Spartacus'. Immediately afterwards, the man next to him stood up and said, '*I* am Spartacus'. The man next to him also stood up and said, 'No, *I* am Spartacus'. Within minutes every one of those conquered slaves was on his feet identifying himself as Spartacus, making it impossible for General Marcus to isolate their leader.

Each man, by standing up, chose death. The loyalty of the group was to a shared vision, inspired by Spartacus, that they could be 'free'. Their vision was so compelling that not a single person in the army was prepared to give it up for slavery. In the midst of adversity the response was a creative one!

A shared vision is more than an idea or feeling, it permeates a person's whole being with a powerful force. Few forces among people are more powerful than a shared vision. It builds commitment and unity. You can probably think of your own example, but Anita Roddick of The Body Shop is one instance of how a sustained vision, shared by others (her employees), has made a difference.

Exceptional individuals and enterprises use their own levels of energy to relentlessly pursue their vision; they have a deep desire to achieve and are continuously looking to improve the way things are. Deep desire seems to be a good thing for themselves as individuals, for others and for society. But desire taken to an extreme can become an obsession and may lead to harm and different types of risks. The author D.H. Lawrence suggested that some people may be too spiritual, some may be too sensual, some may be too sympathetic and some may be too proud.

There is an old proverb that states, 'virtue stands in the middle'. This encourages us to do things in moderation and to temper our desire. Exceptional individuals and enterprises seem to thrive on a strong desire to achieve their vision.

Providing the right conditions

> Democracy encourages the majority to decide things about
> which the majority is blissfully ignorant.
> —John Simon, English statesman

Two prerequisites are needed before thinking critically can flourish in the workplace—the first is a commitment to democracy and the second is a sense of individual freedom. For some of us a lack of self-confidence will mean that it is a challenge to assert our right to express ourselves, to question the way things are done and to explore issues we may not be certain about. The more we explore, the more uncertain we may become, but while the path to thinking critically may mean that we experience a level of humility, the potential reward is increased wisdom. In order to create an environment where inquiry and cooperation go together, where managers are not threatened if staff ask questions or offer alternatives and where staff feel confident to ask those questions, company philosophy needs to embrace the principle of thinking critically and to foster a culture of openness.

Persuade, don't dominate

Here's an example of how a dominating manager had adverse consequences for one business. A long-established hospitality company provided entertainment and gaming facilities using constantly changing technology. Tom, the general manager, was a hard task-master who rigorously monitored his managers' performances. They always had to do exactly what they were told. Tom told them he paid them to deliver the same service every day and he didn't want them changing anything without his permission—they weren't paid to think.

With each upgrade of technology it was necessary for the managers to learn new skills. However, Tom felt there was no time to do any training because they were too busy—a luxury they could ill afford. They had to learn things as they went along and do their best. Without being fully aware of it Tom's domination encouraged his staff to be conditional thinkers, to rely upon him for everything.

This adversely affected the company by creating a debilitating culture: the managers were unable to cope with the introduction of the new technology, which led to stress and unachievable goals. In particular, initiative was assassinated and efficient service was crippled.

Persuasion is different from domination. Sometimes people will invite you to contribute and participate in decision making in order to make you feel as if you have contributed but when it comes down to it, they will exclude your ideas. This is bad business practice. If you try to tell others what to do and impose your will you are not engaging in the spirit of thinking critically.

Many times I have seen young executives participate in courses to learn about management and leadership skills, especially the art of delegation and how to better involve their staff in decision making within their departments. These are good initiatives on the part of the company, but unfortunately they often have a fatal flaw. In most cases these young executives are not involved in actually making decisions, nor is there a culture that encourages them to do so. Moreover, it is clear that the only management practices they would be allowed to adopt would be the ones already in use in their organisation, rather than the new strategies they were learning about. As well, I found that many employees and middle managers were not confident in their reasoning, tended not to look for options to a problem and were not aware of the importance of thinking critically.

Exercises

Personal Encouragement Screening Test (PEST)

Try this test on yourself and then ask different colleagues to answer the same questions about you so you can compare your results with theirs. Do they think you encourage more than you do? What can you learn from this?

Following is a list of 20 statements about encouragement. Read each statement and circle the number that most accurately matches your current behaviour. A rating of 1 indicates that you *never* engage in that behaviour while a rating of 6 indicates that you *always* behave in the manner described.

1	2	3	4	5	6
Never	Hardly ever	Some-times	Often	Nearly always	Always

Circle one number for each statement

1. I help others to influence decisions	1 2 3 4 5 6
2. I encourage others to be leaders	1 2 3 4 5 6
3. I show others I value the everyday routines	1 2 3 4 5 6
4. I openly acknowledge others for their efforts	1 2 3 4 5 6
5. I listen to the stories others tell	1 2 3 4 5 6
6. I share my stories about our work	1 2 3 4 5 6
7. I take time to celebrate small and big events	1 2 3 4 5 6
8. I encourage our group to celebrate successes	1 2 3 4 5 6
9. I am positive towards others in tough times	1 2 3 4 5 6
10. I acknowledge those who take responsibility	1 2 3 4 5 6
11. I share how I work towards my goals	1 2 3 4 5 6
12. I acknowledge people's uniqueness	1 2 3 4 5 6
13. I find new ways to reward people for their efforts	1 2 3 4 5 6
14. I promote job satisfaction	1 2 3 4 5 6
15. I search for new ways to acknowledge others	1 2 3 4 5 6
16. I applaud people regardless of circumstances	1 2 3 4 5 6

17. I let others know that I believe in them   1 2 3 4 5 6
18. I develop helpful human relationships   1 2 3 4 5 6
19. I work productively with others   1 2 3 4 5 6
20. I find better ways for people to cooperate   1 2 3 4 5 6

Add all the scores together to get a total, and use that total to work out your PEST profile.

Score 100–120: **Clever Encourager**—You are able to maintain a healthy and productive environment through the interpersonal skill of encouraging others.

Score 80–99: **Competent Encourager**—You are at a useful level of encouraging others but can learn better ways to encourage more frequently.

Score 60–79: **Cautious Encourager**—You can do many things to improve your capacity to encourage others and achieve results through it.

Score less than 60: **Contra Encourager**—Your score is unlikely to be so low. This level indicates much unhappiness and you may need to seek professional advice.

The self-assessment index of democratic behaviour (SAID-B)

The antidote to mild domination is to try to participate more in the decision-making structure of your company and, if you are in a position to do so, to encourage others. But first you'll need to discover just how democratic *you* are in the workplace. The SAID-B can be a basis for you to focus on improving your own participation and that of others.

Following is a list of 20 statements about workplace democratic behaviours. Read each statement and circle the number that most accurately matches your current behaviour. A rating of 1 indicates that you *never* engage in that behaviour while a rating of 6 indicates that you *always* behave in the manner described.

1	2	3	4	5	6
Never	Hardly ever	Some-times	Often	Nearly always	Always

Circle one number for each statement

1. I encourage a spirit of inquiry when I think it is appropriate   1 2 3 4 5 6
2. I search for opportunities to change and grow   1 2 3 4 5 6
3. I take risks at the expense of making a fool of myself   1 2 3 4 5 6
4. I share my perceptions about the future and what I think we should strive for   1 2 3 4 5 6
5. I try to get others to commit to a shared perception of what we want   1 2 3 4 5 6
6. I am expressive, warm, friendly, gentle, persuasive and enthusiastic   1 2 3 4 5 6
7. I play a leadership development role when it is appropriate   1 2 3 4 5 6
8. I encourage others to cooperate by seeking first to cooperate with them   1 2 3 4 5 6
9. I foster feelings of ownership in others   1 2 3 4 5 6
10. I do things to promote mutual respect, trust, dignity, self-esteem, confidence and capability   1 2 3 4 5 6
11. I openly promote freedom of speech, expression and participation   1 2 3 4 5 6
12. I can choose the best leadership role to play when the situation requires it   1 2 3 4 5 6
13. I tell others about my plans or my intentions, e.g. how I will reach particular goals, to change a particular habit etc.   1 2 3 4 5 6
14. I try to set an example by modelling consistent progress through action   1 2 3 4 5 6
15. I stretch my own goals by raising my own standard for excellence   1 2 3 4 5 6

16. I offer to act as a support and thinking
    partner/mentor to others   1 2 3 4 5 6
17. I invite others to lead, e.g. a seminar, a
    project   1 2 3 4 5 6
18. I bring together an excellent combination of
    people to work on issues   1 2 3 4 5 6
19. I tell others who my coach and mentor are
    and the sorts of things I learn from them   1 2 3 4 5 6
20. I brainstorm with my colleagues on ways to
    encourage, involve, support and champion   1 2 3 4 5 6

Add all the scores together to get a total and use that total to see how well you rated.

Score 100–120: You often strive in many ways to maintain healthy and productive relationships through encouraging freedom of expression, participation and mutual support.

Score 60–99: You are at a useful level of encouraging productive relationships but can learn better ways to promote freedom and participation more frequently.

Score less than 60: You can do many additional things to improve your capacity to encourage others and achieve results through it.

> There are high spots in all of our lives and most of them have come about through encouragement from someone else.
> I don't care how great, how famous or successful a man or woman may be, each hungers for applause.
> —George M. Adams, American statesman

Key 4 Think critically in a group

Never doubt that a small group of thoughtful committed people can change the world: indeed it's the only thing that ever has!

—Margaret Mead, anthropologist

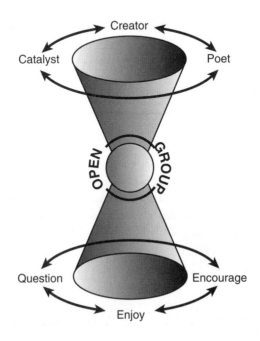

The hourglass model of thinking critically spins around one central hub, the open group. Most writers on the topic of thinking critically rarely talk about thinking critically in a group or in a team. The focus is usually on the individual, yet teamwork can lead to empowerment on a personal level. It is generally recognised that we cannot but learn from the moment we are born to the moment we die. Proximity to others leads to an understanding of the self. One way in which we all achieve this to some degree is through formal learning: school and university. Informal and incidental learning is very powerful and also occurs through social and cultural processes.

In addition to mastering these individual and group competencies those keen to master thinking critically would do well to adhere to structures of adult learning principles that encourage independence, autonomy and self actualisation. Encouraging people to understand why they are learning something, the bigger picture, is in itself a group thinking critically activity. Consider three employees who have returned from a day of training. The manager asks two questions: 'What did you learn today? Why did you go to training?' The first is a basic question requiring simple recall and the response will indicate a level of comprehension by the employees. The second is a question that evokes thinking critically, giving an opportunity for the employees to make links between learning content/skills, their own individual development and the strategic direction of the enterprise.

The conversation about the questions can be a tremendous encouragement process for a group. The nature of the responses will give clear indications about each employee's capacity to have a strategic focus on their own training. Say the first employee answers, 'Ahh, let's see. I learned things, you know and I went because you said I had to go'. This is a vague answer and the motivation is one of just following a management directive. The second employee may say, 'Ahh, I learned things like, hmm . . . oh yes, communication skills and a whole lot of stuff like that, and I loved it. I went because you said I would get paid for it and after all it was a day away from my job'. This response is also vague and general and the motivation is an enjoyable day away from the coal-face at the company's expense! The third employee might say, 'I learned things like . . . communication skills. I really got a lot out of the coaching skills and I have some new tips on how to give other staff constructive feedback, especially on-the-job. I've come to realise how important my job is to helping the company advance. I know that by simply doubling the number of times I encourage other staff daily (giving them constructive feedback) I will greatly improve our approach. I went because I know we are currently rolling out a new strategic direction for our company and I realise that I have an important role to play in helping to build the teamwork so we can give superior service to our customers and achieve our vision of being "their first choice".' This is a well-focused and useful answer showing the employee's appreciation of his or her role in the organisation.

Thinking staff who can articulate connections between their individual learning and their role in the company as a part of a group are every manager's desire. This type of conversation is also a way of fostering adults to use their experience to learn. The meaning of being an adult is being self-directed, responsible for your own decision making and actions, and achieving an interdependent independence. Purposeful conversation supports people in being task-centred, whole-oriented and solutions focused. The most potent motivators are the intrinsic ones which keep you growing and the internal pressures to achieve a complete quality of life, self-esteem and a sense of personal satisfaction. We need to figure these patterns into the structure of mastering thinking critically at a group level.

The whole is greater than the sum of its parts

> My grandfather once told me that there are two kinds of people: those who work and those who take the credit. He told me to try to be in the first group; there was less competition there.
> —Indira Gandhi, former Prime Minister of India

There is strength in numbers. One piece of paper is too flimsy to hold much weight, but if you put two pieces of paper together, one under the other, they will bear much more weight than could be held by each separately. This principle is put into practice in a safety procedure used by the Australian Federal Police: a box containing several reams of paper is used as a buffer when armed police unload their guns at the end of a shift. Should a gun discharge accidentally, the bullet would be stopped effectively by the layers of paper.

A team can only work well if everyone pulls their weight and is willing to take an equal share of the load and responsibility. Each member should be able to identify with each other in the pursuit of their goals in a way that shows they are all accountable for the outcome. Consider your hand a group of five fingers and a palm representing a team. Each finger is unique, like a person, possessing complementary skills—for example, the thumb performs those opposable tasks ensuring the grip is firm while the index finger has its pointing, poking and fossicking function. Each is of a different breadth, length and strength yet indispensable when refining performance. Only when they work together, committed to a common purpose, a common approach and accountable to each other for their part, is the execution of the goal likely to be perfectly successful.

A team that has a comprehensive mix of talents has a greater chance of success and innovation, as well as problem-solving abilities. Ideally, team members would have complementary skills, like a hand. Diversity and heterogeneity support innovation and creativity. An effective management strategy for building a team would be to value members with differences, to respect them, to build on strengths and to compensate for weaknesses. Communication is the glue that binds team member differences. When this happens, the result is something creative.

Synergy among human beings is something we know little about, although its existence is widely acknowledged. Put simply, synergy is a group energy that is greater than the sum of the contribution of its individual members. Synergy is the ultimate objective on the path of thinking critically in a group. A team is said to achieve synergy when it is free of negative forms of group dynamics such as defensiveness, jealousy, domination and hatred. Sometimes I wonder if it is necessary to have the absolute absence of these undesirable dynamics, perhaps we should aim for a robust group that has the capacity to manage them productively. In extreme and overpowering quantities these emotions will overpower and destroy, but when harnessed properly they can provide invaluable energy.

The result of synergy between human beings is creativity. In order to achieve synergy, the members of a group need a mindset of expecting challenge as a healthy, inviting and productive way to interrelate.

Diversity and thinking critically in a group

> On a group of theories one can found a school; but on a
> group of values one can found a culture, a civilization, a new
> way of living together among people.
> —Ignazio Silone, Italian politician and author

Thinking critically starts with the individual but is tested in the group. The group element becomes a vital part of the process—it is where an individual's rhetoric is put to trial. The social aspects of a group are very useful in developing critical thinking skills. Working on your own is one thing but pitting yourself against the group requires disciplined application. For everyone, a mixture of individual and group work would seem ideal.

Many people need quiet time to generate ideas, to identify assumptions, to think through an approach and to mull over alternatives to an idea. These ideas can then be taken to the group to develop even further. Thinking critically does not have to occur in a group because an individual can both generate and develop an idea, but where it does occur in a cooperative group intent on friendly adversity the result is likely to be enhanced. Since the basis of thinking critically is 'openness' there is no better structure than that of a group with a diversity of members.

Diversity is about people and their relationship to each other, to their jobs, to society's institutions, to the nation and to the world. Diversity is a strategic issue for both communities and for business. This means that people formulate goals, take a long-term view, a global view of living and working, and relate that view to a 'bigger picture'. A focus on diversity offers different choices to organisations facing a range of circumstances. Differences in goals often reflect differences in people's basic values and the meaning they ascribe to key words such as achievement, success and productivity. There are no off-the-shelf formulas for organisations concerned with diversity. However, the community and business world can seek to activate tailored and dynamic changes that take into account a diverse population and workforce.

Diversity refers to differences among the members of a group, an organisation, a nation or the world. Common usage of the word diversity refers to differences in demographic attributes such as race, ethnicity, gender, age, physical status, religion, education or sexual orientation. Another way to look at differences is that there are differences in kind—that is, innate differences such as gender and race—and differences in degree, such as economic status.

Differences in degree are socially constructed whereas innate or genetic differences are not, even though their descriptions are. Both types of differences constitute diversity. Differences in nature or nurture, however, are not in themselves a sufficient basis for classifying the difference as an asset or as a disadvantage. People discriminate unfairly when they begin to equate difference with deficiency. Valuing diversity means that people start to display a willingness to accept in other people values and behaviours which are dissimilar from their own. In this sense diversity becomes a practical skill and attitude.

Diversity is a process of acknowledging differences in the ways we interact. This means that the quality of interactions among work and social groups, the relationships between managers and employees or among friends, and the structures which shape or channel people's actions will be welcoming of heterogeneity. We welcome diversity because it is the right thing to do. There are also pragmatic and compelling factors, such as the economic imperative and the shift in demographics, that have resulted in greater diversity in communities and in the workforce. This means that organisations that foster diversity seem to be the ones that have a competitive advantage.

Diversity gives an organisation competitive advantage because all of its people are empowered—that is, they know that they can influence the direction of the organisation—they share respect for each other, they share a clarity about their common purpose, they develop their capabilities to act and they give and receive acknowledgment and recognition for their contributions. In other words, irrespective of their differences, everyone in a community or organisation has equal opportunities. Both the moral and economic imperatives share a dialectical relationship in the rhetoric on valuing diversity in the workplace.

Diversity is a group-based idea. Therefore, effective solutions can best be sought on a group or team basis because learning occurs at *both* the individual and group levels. Put another way, people that value diversity raise their chances of being effective because valuing diversity means respecting the different approaches to work that people have and learning to harness these differences for the benefit of the team. When we make new or revised interpretations of the meaning of an experience we can say we have learned. This learning then acts as a guide to our subsequent understanding, appreciation and ways of acting.

Creating hype for a team helps the diversity of membership to become cohesive, as exciting experiences are often bonding experiences. Creating cohesion in a group is essential for team performance. Cohesion helps members tolerate each other's differences and even enjoy them. A cohesive group is likely to tolerate a 'black sheep' as a member, whereas the same behaviour outside the group would be deemed unacceptable.

Encouraging interaction among people destined to be team members with others; reassurance and support from key executives, consultants or significant others; allowing time for individual members to voice their concerns about the intended direction as well as offering detailed information, are ways that foster commitment and diversity. Creating a climate to deal with resistance without killing diversity involves setting the stage upon which resistance expressed in the form of fear, perceived alienation, politics or concerns about future can be dissipated. Showing respect for, and empathising with feelings of resistance, promoting communication to minimise the deleterious effects of gossiping, and encouraging participation, are some proven strategies for successfully encouraging diversity and dealing with resistance to change.

Groupthink

While it is important for group members to share a cooperative spirit, it's also important to be aware of the danger of too much cohesion. It may lead to a phenomenon called *groupthink*. Groupthink can exist in a group as small as two people. Close friends, for example, who share similar beliefs and prejudices, are prone to fall into the groupthink trap. Friendship differences dissolve to pale homogeneity, a type of emotional correspondence I call 'group-feel'. In a work-related group, team members who share a high degree of interpersonal beliefs are in danger of holding a distorted view of a situation. Groupthink can lead to faulty decision making and problem solving as members rush to a consensus so they can maintain 'group-feel' and avoid conflict.

Thinking critically in groups is an effective way to dissolve the effects of groupthink. If you are coordinating a group in which everyone agrees to a single proposition, challenge it. Ask people to go away and come back when they can explain the idea from a different perspective and when they can offer options that are just as good. Such options do exist in all cases. In this sense, routinely identifying and challenging assumptions of team members becomes an expected way of operating.

Tackling group bias

A bias is the weight in the side of a bowling ball that ensures the ball comes to rest on that side. A bias in our thinking is the weight we put on a previous experience that ensures our current action falls in line with the previous experience. When this happens, our decisions come to rest on that side of our bias. There are two types of bias: heuristics and thinking traps.

A heuristic is a method used in problem solving that relies on inductive reasoning from past experience. Some people are able to use heuristics simply and effectively while others allow their past experiences to totally influence their decisions. For instance, 'This is the only solution I'm prepared to consider because it's worked for me in the past.' There are two types of heuristics, memory and attachment. *Memory heuristics* are slightly more impersonal, mainly a recollection of an event, external to the individual. The emotional element varies in intensity but is usually diluted. *Attachment heuristics* are more emotional, more meaningful and internal to the individual. Rather than the memory of an event, it is the emotional fire-storm that drives these heuristics.

Thinking traps also come in two types: confirmation and hindsight. Confirmation thinking traps are where someone seeks confirmation for what they already think is true and avoids opportunities to search out disconfirming information. Hindsight thinking traps are where someone exaggerates the extent to which they could have anticipated an event.

Heuristics

First, let's clarify the similarities and differences between the two types of heuristics. Both involve reminiscing to different degrees and both have an emotional element, but the intensity varies with each type of heuristic. Memory heuristics have more to do with a recall or 'past history' that still includes an emotional element but usually less intense than an attachment heuristic. Attachment heuristics are emotional nets firmly secured within an individual. Emotions accumulated and confined through reminiscing or having past ties with a person, place or thing are what create the bias in attachment heuristics. Of course, when both heuristics exist in tandem the bias created tends to be very strong and more difficult to recognise and overcome.

Let's take planning as an example of a heuristic in action and see how different approaches can produce different outcomes. Ideally, a project is started with a firm idea of the outcomes to be achieved. Once there is an idea, strategies for action will begin to emerge. Unfortunately, some people spend very little or no time creating their vision. They get stuck on a single perspective and forget that other approaches have benefits. A process approach is an alternative to an outcomes mindset. You do not start a project with a firm idea of the outcomes in mind. You take a 'goal-free' approach. This means that rather than relying on working backwards from firm outcomes, you work through an established procedure diligently noting approaches as they occur, cataloguing the benefits as they reveal themselves and enjoying the apparent chaos that typically surrounds a process mindset.

How heuristics and thinking traps affect thinking critically in a group

Much of group discussion involves group members sharing memories of past experiences and their attachment to those experiences. Interpretative sharing of experience is filled with personal bias and aims to gain from group members both confirmation and validation of the nature and success of those experiences. Both heuristics and thinking traps work against a group's pursuit of thinking critically because they involve strong and hidden individual biases that need to be identified and challenged.

Alternatively, heuristics and thinking traps can be a creative springboard to thinking critically in a group. This occurs where members have a commitment to building on experiences and attachments by extending them to various bizarre conclusions to see what will happen. When we do this we adopt a poetic response to heuristics and thinking traps (see the section on 'Use of language' in Key 6, 'Become a poet'.)

A helpful guide to any group's decision making might be to acknowledge memories and past experiences that members have in relation to the issue at hand as the first step. This acknowledgement is not too dissimilar from declaring a conflict of interest in the issue because of past experiences.

Thinking traps

There are many dynamics in a group that mitigate against open discussion and decision making. No factors are so powerful and subtle as the thinking traps of seeking confirmation for your own ideas, interests and preferences and for your own skill and capacity to get results. I am not talking about simple manipulation of one another in subtle ways but what many people believe to be honest approaches to achieving what they, themselves think is best. After all, wolves lose their teeth but not their nature. This is the nature of group interaction—to seek confirmation and validation of your own personal experiences, interests and thoughts.

So there are two naturally occurring types of thinking traps: confirmation and hindsight. A clue to positively maximise their effects is to remember that a big drum sounds good only from a distance. Wanting confirmation is like wanting to be a big drum. The way to sound good is to be appreciated from a distance, dispassionately. When you openly promote others' ideas you are distancing yourself from your own ideas in the first instance.

Of course, thinking traps serve a very useful purpose. They are part of the engine that drives the group. Imagine if there were no personal interests and no desire to be accepted for your ideas and for your capabilities. It would mean a lack of energy in the group and, through boredom, the possible abandonment of any sort of group effort. Our nature is to be gregarious and part of how we achieve this is to seek out approval for our ideas and capabilities. The struggles people experience in a group should not be avoided but enjoyed. Verbal combat in a group is needed to extract the benefits of thinking traps. Think of a group as a contest among the members as well as a contest between the members in the group and others outside the group. Friendly but fierce combat is what achieves progress. Machiavelli offers advice on how groups work. He says there are two ways to conduct a contest: one by law and the other by force. In a group, the law is the explicit rules established to conduct a group, involving taking turns, equity in talking and cooperating. But the law is often not stated or not clear on how particular groups will be conducted. Of course, force in a group also can be explicit and implicit. When you openly assert your power you are being explicit but when you are subtly seeking confirmation and compliance you are using a subtle power of domination. This is the nature of thinking traps. In struggles for power, people's judgements are often entirely based on self-interest and finding a direct and economical pathway to *your* own personal goal. You do what *you* have to do! Numero uno, you, is what counts.

Exercises

Confirmation thinking traps

Try the following exercise with a group of friends or colleagues. Sit in a circle and take turns to identify personal experiences where you or others are asked to have a decision confirmed without knowing if it had been investigated or explored.

Examples could include:

- We need to refurnish our offices.
- We need to hire more staff.
- We will be having our holiday in Vanuatu instead of Bali.
- We have postponed the party, okay?
- We have cut the invitation list by 20 per cent.

Group critical thinking

This exercise works best with twelve people formed into six teams of two. When creating a team it is important to bear in mind any complementary skills and knowledge among potential team members— try to create a mixture of people who can each bring something specific to the task at hand. A team that has a good mix of talents has a greater chance of success and innovative capability, as well as potentially greater problem-solving abilities.

Each of the six pairs will be given a Team number and name as follows.

Team 1: Issues team—openly discusses an issue for 10 minutes

Team 2: Subjective team—identifies the explicit assumptions and points of view and asks the Issues team to identify others omitted

Team 3: Objective team—identifies the implicit assumptions and points of view and asks about assumptions outside the Issues team

Team 4: Ideas team—lists the key issues discussed, groups them into themes and then asks the Issues team about their logic and creativity

Team 5: Emotions team—identifies patterns in the ways of feelings among the Issues team and asks about other emotions not identified

Team 6: Helicopter team—observes and comments on the whole event, especially the comments made by the member of Teams two, three, four and five.

This process relies on full and open participation and discussion by the six teams. The focus is on openness, empathy and listening. The Issues team discuss a problem or issue while the other teams listen and observe from the pre-defined perspective of their team. After the Issues team has completed its discussion, each team takes it in turns to give information and feedback and to ask questions of the Issues team. The interaction among teams should be characterised by openness, cooperation and non-defensive behaviours. It is important for each team to stick to its prescribed areas of obser-vation and reporting.

The Subjective team identifies the explicit assumptions and points of view and asks the Issues team to identify others omitted as well as describing any examples of openness and valuing difference and the types of communication behaviours witnessed among any Issues team members. The Objective team identifies the implicit assumptions and points of view and asks about assumptions outside the Issues team—for example, from the point of view of a parent, a child, the economy, politics, the environment, from a competitive advantage perspective or from a stakeholder's point of view. The Ideas team lists the key issues discussed, groups them into themes and then asks the Issues team about their logic and creativity. The Emotions team identifies patterns in the ways of feelings among the Issues team and asks about other emotions not identified. Finally, the Helicopter team gets to comment on its observations of the entire discussion and all interactions. It comments on the whole event, especially the participation of teams two, three, four and five.

To decrease complexity it is possible to reduce the number of teams that will observe and comment. It is useful to allow each team a few moments to discuss their team's observations before they report them and ask questions about them. The final debrief can address the question of what was learned, the insights gained and what implications there are for action, for personal growth and for community and organisational development.

A group-based strategy such as the one described here encourages people to identify different perspectives within context, to question them, to suggest alternatives and to empower individuals to decide what to do if anything. Group-based strategies raise awareness of difference of diversity and of ways of behaving which are the bases for recognising that change can be powerful.

How to avoid groupthink

To find out how your group feels about the way in which thinking critically is encouraged, ask each member to agree or disagree with the following statements.

1. We challenge consensus when it is used to disguise conflict.
2. We convert conformity into generating options.
3. We challenge unilateral decisions after they are made.
4. We identify expedient arguments.
5. We ask about personal agendas.
6. We encourage individuals to express inner tensions as group members.
7. We praise mutual scrutiny and evaluation so that members explore options.
8. We promote fantasy and expressions of emotions in the group.
9. We question everything.
10. We check frequently that group participation is not a shrewd form of control.

If there is consensus on all ten questions within the group, what does that tell you about groupthink in your particular network? You may be surprised to find that the answers reveal widespread groupthink, indicating that your group is unconsciously incompetent in its development. How healthy do you think it is to reach consensus without having explored multiple perspectives? Quiet time perhaps is needed to think, imagine and dream a little more.

Identifying heuristics

The focus of these exercises will be on questioning the judgement of the person who made the decision; remember: the heuristics are tools for making judgements.

Find a colleague who can be a critical friend and who can challenge your thinking and your decisions and try the following activities together. The smallest group you can have, two people, is a useful, non-threatening place to start exploring biases. The purpose of this exercise is to raise awareness of a memory heuristic that will have biased a decision. The aim is to uncover bias in a decision emanating from your memory of a past experience.

1. Ask a colleague or friend to identify a decision they made recently that was influenced by a similar past event. For example, they may have (dis)approved the development of a new product because they experienced success (or failure) with a similar one in the past.

2. What is similar about the two events? How did the past event (failure/success) influence the present decision? Were the products similar? Were the circumstances similar? Were the customers, the location, the political and social structures similar?

3. What is different about the current context and decision compared to the past ones?

4. The aim is to uncover bias inherent in one's memory. Are there good reasons to maintain the bias?

5. To decrease the memory bias, generate together a set of three criteria to guide a similar type of decision in the future. How else can you diminish this bias?

Attachment heuristic

The aim of this exercise is to raise awareness of a simple attachment heuristic that may have biased a decision. Ask a colleague to listen carefully to three incidents and to help you to identify the patterns or attachment heuristic.

Here are three incidents:

1. I hired a manager because he had a degree from the university where I got my degree.

2. I approve site visits to anywhere in New Zealand because I have lived and worked there and I love the place.
3. I agreed to fund that particular community group because I used to be a volunteer there for many years and I have a soft spot for it.

Now articulate your own incidents:

1. _____
2. _____
3. _____

Your colleague should comment about whether your decisions are biased by your attachments. The aim is to uncover possible bias inherent in your attachments. Is it reasonable to allow your attachments to guide your decisions?

To tackle any attachment bias, generate another set of three criteria to guide that type of decision in the future, in particular by focusing on the needs of the group.

Try the following exercise with a group of friends or colleagues. Sit in a circle and take turns with your colleagues or friends to identify personal experiences or events where you or others have predicted accurately what will happen before it actually occurred. For example, the increase in revenue by x per cent over a specific time period; we knew that Frederick and Michaela would not come to the party.

1. List predicted events and try and allocate a percentage level of confidence in each prediction. For example, an absolute certainty would be 100 per cent.
2. Support your level of confidence by sharing with the group the reasons that you regard as excellent reasons for the successful prediction.
3. Encourage the group to quantify or suggest the extent to which you could have overestimated the predicted event actually occurring: e.g. highly likely (90–100% chance), likely (50–89%), unlikely (15–49%), highly unlikely (less than 15%).

Become a catalyst

A great many people think they are thinking when they are merely rearranging their prejudices.
—William James, philosopher and psychologist

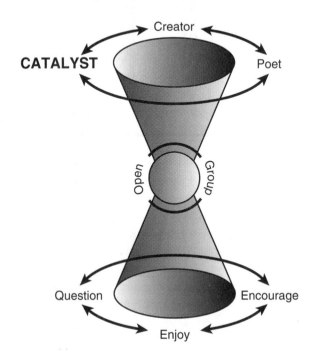

Reasoning is something that is quite easy to take for granted in everyday life. When we get stuck trying to work out a problem we can find ourselves going around in circles, perhaps feeling more isolated and deluded by the absence of a satisfactory solution. In many situations when people get stuck trying to decipher an issue they do not think to think about how they are using their reasoning skills. Are they challenging themselves or allowing the problem to overwhelm them and submitting to defeat?

A catalyst is an agitator, a chemical that reacts and causes change without itself being changed. It is a substance, such as an enzyme, that enables a chemical reaction to proceed at a faster rate or under different conditions, such as at a lower temperature, than otherwise possible. Enzymes, types of chemicals such as anti-oxidants, are naturally occurring catalysts responsible for many essential biochemical reactions. I am using the term catalyst to mean a person that provokes or speeds significant change or action. This is a person who is able to be the spark, to create other sparks and provoke interest, energy and movement.

The biggest obstacle to catalysts is authority. You might refer to this type of authority as catalyst poison, an attitude that reduces the effectiveness of a catalyst in the workplace. In theory, because catalyst persons are not consumed in chemical reactions in the events they spark off, they can do this repeatedly over an indefinite period of time. To become a natural catalyst you simply need to first start a reaction. You need to be provocative, to twitch the minds around you. Only then can you keep the process of critical reasoning going.

Of course, you can be a catalyst to yourself or to others. Some ways to provoke a situation are to propose questions/ideas that:

- introduce uncertainty: for example, Am I sure about that? Are you sure about that?
- deny reality: for example, There is no such thing as bad customers, profits, efficiency etc.
- upset the time-line: for example, It will never happen. It will take too long. What if it starts tomorrow?
- shake it, move it, taste it, smell it, borrow it, take it with you, push it to its limit etc.

- introduce a random idea and expect the others to make sense of it: for example, It's like a banana.
- insist on piloting: for example, I'll (let's) give it a go now. I'll (let's) play with that before we decide.

You might recall the example in Key 2 of a prison that needed to be upgraded to accommodate one hundred more inmates. The authorities gave instructions to surround the quadrangle with an inner security fence that would cost $100 000. It would probably sound absurd if you heard someone say, 'Why don't you just draw a thick white line instead?' Yet this statement is an apt example of being a catalyst. It would cause emotional reaction and intellectual rejection, the motion that would then be the basis for critical analysis of challenging assumptions. We know that in this case this was the best solution accepted for a hundredth of the cost, $1000.

Another example is a company that wanted to build a new laboratory to house powerful X-ray gear to examine castes and forgings for concealed blemishes. The drawing of the laboratory included a concrete wall over 2 metres thick and 5 metres high in the shape of a horseshoe outside the building to protect the adjacent areas from radiation. How could you become a catalyst in this situation? You might say, 'What an ugly idea!' This provocation could lead to a creative discussion. Would an especially padded foil do the job? What about a wall of soil? Advice from the engineers showed how unusual it was to include this much idle concrete that didn't even bear a load. The catalyst comment led to a key question, 'What else will stop radiation?' The advice came back that a mound of dirt 5 metres thick and 5 metres high would do the job. This was less than a tenth of the cost of the concrete wall and had many advantages, especially its easy removability if the laboratory needed to be relocated.

Catalyst poisons are those attitudes and responses from others that you need to avoid and actively reject because they will extinguish your spark. When you are always sparking, just like spark plugs inside an engine, you create movement so all those that are connected to you will move as well. One spark sets off another one and you can create light and movement until the direction becomes clear to you. The catalyst poisons to avoid include:

- rejecting new ideas or suggestions by staff
- always sticking to your knitting (doing the things you feel safe with)
- organising a committee to examine an idea
- inviting specialists to give you a business plan
- discussing something for a year
- being inert and stable! Stability without provocation is anti-critical and anti-creative.

Rather, be bold, get some movement going, see what happens when you try it, how others respond, who likes, dislikes, who helps and if anyone will champion the idea. For example, suggest your company allocates multiple small grants, incentives to set people in motion to trial ideas in relatively short periods, say at one to two monthly periods. Tell people you will pay them a few hundred dollars if they visit other organisations and bring back an idea or two and give their colleagues a short talk on what they discovered. Create hype and interest; increase the amount of talk in your company and establish a new habit, a hive of activity.

> The greatest revolution in our generation is that of human beings, who by changing the inner attitudes of their minds, can change the outer aspects of their lives.
> —Marilyn Ferguson, editor, publisher and award-winning author of *The Aquarian Conspiracy*

In today's world, change is pervasive. The information technology revolution happening now is forcing people to work differently. Many people are required to work with new technology and for this to happen effectively they need support. It is not helpful to simply establish goals and action plans under these new conditions and then expect others to sink or swim. Helping them to adapt to their changing environment, to make decisions for themselves and to play a beneficial role in their company can be accomplished if managers act as catalysts.

How one company changed

SEMCO manufactures a varied range of products, including pumps that can empty oil tankers overnight, dishwashers that clean over 4100 plates every hour, air conditioners, mixers that blend almost anything, including rocket fuel and chewing gum, and mammoth biscuit factories. It is Brazil's largest marine and food processing machinery manufacturer. It's not what SEMCO makes that has earned it an international reputation but rather how it operates. Ricardo Semler, CEO of the renowned company, is a catalyst. He says that success for him is when others are making the decisions. He doesn't like to be called 'boss', he prefers the term 'counsellor'.

SEMCO was a traditional organisation in every respect when Ricardo Semler took over the business from his father. It had the usual pyramid structure and a rule for every contingency with an entrenched hierarchy and a conservative approach. Everyone was as starched as their shirts. Antonio, Ricardo's father, was born in Austria in 1912 and worked as a production engineer in a chemical and textile plant until he went to Brazil and secured a patent for a centrifuge that could separate lubricating oil from vegetables. Father and son did not get on at all when Ricardo started work there. Antonio was a traditionalist who treated his employees paternalistically and considered strikes as personal affronts. His routine was highly predictable and impeccable. He demanded respect and instilled fear with a stern look being his trademark. He disliked many of Ricardo's habits such as putting his feet on his desk, using office resources for personal reasons, working from home and preferring to be called Dickie instead of Dr Ricardo. There was a 50-year gap between father and son and their styles and ideas were very incompatible, which was compounded when the Brazilian economy went into reverse. By 1980, Brazil's marine industry was hard hit and about 90 per cent of SEMCO business was in marine products and pumps. The only profits being generated were from investments of cash reserves.

Finally, Antonio handed ownership to Ricardo, saying that it was better Ricardo makes his mistakes while Antonio was still alive.

Then Antonio left for a two-week holiday. Ricardo wanted to diversify SEMCO and the first thing he did was to interview all executives with the intention of firing them. 'Does your father know about this?' was the question they asked. Ricardo fired 60 per cent of SEMCO's top executives. He needed emergency surgery not slow herbal treatment. Ricardo then proceeded to turn SEMCO into something entirely different—a result that his father was most unhappy about.

These are some of the radical ideas Semler implemented. Staff at SEMCO now set their own production quotas and even go into work in their own time to meet the quotas without any prodding from management and without overtime pay. The factory workers help redesign the products and prepare the marketing plans. The managers have extraordinary freedom to run the business without any interference from the top, they even set their own salaries with no strings. Everyone knows everyone else's salaries and financial information is openly discussed. In fact, there is unlimited access to the books (the union taught everyone to read balance sheets and cash flow statements so that all staff could fully understand the financial side of the business). All employees now have an equal say in how the company is run. For example, when there was a decision to be made about purchasing a new company everyone hopped on a bus and went to inspect the site. The workers made the decision about the purchase.

The SEMCO factory in Brazil consists of four floors of glass and steel with a magnificent reception desk but no receptionist! SEMCO is the most visited company in the world and you need to arrange a long way ahead for a tour. Yet everyone manages their own visitors. No one has secretaries or personal assistants. Everyone pulls their own weight in fetching guests, photocopying and sending faxes and letters. The mood is informal and those who want to can wear suits while those who prefer to dress more casually go for jeans and sneakers. The sales manager, Rubin Agater, sits and reads the paper daily for hours; of course, much of it is information needed for his job. Even so, in most workplaces this would not be tolerated but at SEMCO Rubin keeps abreast of the news and springs into action to more than meet his responsibilities when he judges best.

Ricardo mainly works from home, which means that others can share his office. He encourages other managers to work from home too. Ricardo wanted everyone at SEMCO to be self-sufficient. He didn't like the way that, in the past, decisions depended on particular individuals. So when he takes his two months of holidays every year he roams far without his mobile and he does not call in.

The role of intuition

Money is always there, but the pockets change.
—Gertrude Stein, author

Intuition can play an important role in the process of becoming a catalyst. It is the capacity to make sense of something through your random thoughts, feelings, hunches and insights without relying on logic. Intuition is using your whole mind or body without a conscious effort to think or feel. It is a way of noticing something, then later being able to make sense of it by linking it to something meaningful in your life. It's the sixth sense beyond seeing, touching, tasting, smelling, hearing, yet it includes any of these as well as any of your mental capacities of remembering, reasoning, conceptualising, imagining and your feelings.

Intuition is a random input, a stimulus that comes to you through your senses and mind, which might be knowledge, information, a picture, a smell, sound or a sensation of some other kind that gives you a sense of the pulse of the something else you are thinking about. Intuition is like feeling the heartbeat of the issue you are dealing with, hearing the blood flow and touching the muscular tensions in the problems of your focus, or seeing how the life force is operating in the exchanges you are having. Intuition is sensing the rhythms of our different environments.

Your intuition comes from within you; it is part of your 'gut feelings' rather than originating from stimuli outside of yourself. Intuition begins with a particular self-awareness and then the body interfaces with the environment and the two melt in a way that is sensible. When you touch the environment you start to make sense of your intuition because you are sensing beyond the normal reaches that your body can probe. When you open yourself up to your intuition you are creating a new type of movement and creating fertile ground for critical thinking, for seeing from different perspectives.

Here are some suggestions for enhancing your skills as a catalyst:

1. Immerse yourself in others' projects—and be yourself.
2. Listen in a way that helps other people to understand themselves better.
3. Ask questions to help clarify hidden aspects of an issue in different ways.
4. Identify hidden assumptions and challenge them by posing ambiguities.
5. Make provocative statements that lead to additional insights.
6. Help people to search for solutions, not just one answer.
7. Help others to balance their feelings and thoughts in order to balance intuition and analysis.
8. Help people to shift their way of doing things so they develop new habits.
9. Help others to discover the flaws in thinking logically.

The value of ambiguity

> The awareness of the ambiguity of one's highest achievements (as well as one's deepest failures) is a definite symptom of maturity.
> —Paul Tillich, theologian and philosopher

Hold your open hand, palm facing away from you, about 10 centimetres in front of your face with your fingers spread. Now slowly close each finger into your palm except for one, then focus carefully on that finger, noticing the detail, the clarity, the folds in the skin, the length and shape, the nail and the proportion of patterns. Now look past this finger and focus on the wall or an object several metres behind your finger. What do you notice? You will gradually see that you can still see your finger in the foreground, except now there appear to be two fingers! You have created a different perspective and a rational basis for being a catalyst, using absurdity to reject reality.

If you hold up one finger and ask a colleague how many fingers they see, they will say one. You can reply with some seemingly absurd answer, 'No, I can see two'. You can be provocative and catalytic. You have an explanation and probably they don't. When you are a catalyst, in most cases no one will have an explanation—the challenge is to find one to justify the seemingly absurd comment.

Absurdity is ambiguity gone too far, to a ridiculous, incongruous and unreasonable extent. Some people find this quite difficult to relate to so they manifest the view that there is no order or value in human reality, they exist in a meaningless, irrational world, where there isn't much purpose or meaning. It is interesting that the word 'absurd' derives from the Latin word *surdus*, meaning deaf or muffled and *ab*, to turn away. When things are absurd it means that you turned a deaf ear, things are too silly and you don't want to listen or to understand.

It is the absurd statements that lead to profound critical thinking and inventions. For example, someone might say to you, 'That person was born profoundly deaf and will never hear'. You put on your catalyst personage and respond, 'What total nonsense'. Obviously, a lot of people would probably think you were crazy, but you could then proceed to tell them about an Australian scientist, Graeme Clark from the University of Melbourne, who released in 1979, an implement he created over an eighteen-year period, called the cochlear implant. It helps the profoundly deaf and hearing impaired to hear again. Electrical stimulation to the nerves in the shell-shaped inner ear, the cochlea, allows hearing to function. This 'bionic ear' has helped more than 20 000 people, including 10 000 children in 30 countries to hear.

Imagine then, in the year 2050 some young children may be playing on the floor in a house and an adult tells them to get away from the power-point lest they electrocute themselves. Someone challenges with the catalyst comment, 'Nonsense'. This is because in 1981 the Australian firm Gerard Industries developed a power-point with an in-built electronic circuit that cuts power if there is a power leakage and virtually eliminates the chance of electric shock. By 2050 current powerpoints could very well be illegal and replaced by this sophisticated safety system.

The real skill in becoming a catalyst is actually being provocative without knowing there are existing solutions. You need the confidence that exists in the above examples of knowing solutions exist. In other words, being a catalyst is essentially an attitude of believing there are always solutions within the grasp of our critical and creative thinking and that we simply need to access them.

A man and his wife walk into a second-hand car yard to purchase a car or van that could safely accommodate seven members of the family. They see a van that can seat nine people and inquire about the price—$32 000. The husband is tempted and the wife thinks it will do the job. She makes an offer of $4000 and the salesperson responds in amazement. 'You've got to be joking!' The wife tells him, 'Sorry, this is all we can afford. Here's our phone number if you change your mind'. When they leave the man whispers to his wife, 'That was a rash move; now we've lost it'. Two weeks later the salesman rings and says they can have the van for the price they offered. Of course, it is too late, they have found a better deal. Fear and greed have no place in becoming a catalyst. You have to be prepared to be provocative and move on.

Imagine you are in a similar situation to Ricardo Semler. How certain would you be that you could pull it off? Can you imagine the ambiguity and uncertainty that people around you would initially feel? You would be upsetting their entire world. I'll let you into a secret: Ricardo was an effective catalyst because he had a strong level of an essential quality called *sfumato*. *Sfumato* is an Italian word that means 'all smoked out' or 'gone up in smoke'. If you are *sfumato* you have turned yourself into a mist. As smoke or mist you can float easily through the ether of ambiguity. You are secure within the uncertainty, which is a sign of maturity. This is another way of saying you have confidence in yourself and your ideas and a high tolerance for ambiguity and uncertainty. The challenge of becoming a catalyst is to remain resolute, focused and poised to deal with the growing uncertainty that the reactions around you will create.

Some people maintain that this quality is only found in geniuses such as Leonardo da Vinci, who had access to much wider knowledge than most of his compatriots. However, in this age of the global transmission of information this is a skill that any person who aspires to think critically must master. In the twenty-first century, ambiguity reproduces itself at alarming rates and illusions of certainty are extraordinarily difficult to sustain. If you possess *sfumato* you won't be bewildered by chaos. Instead, you'll discover structure and order in chaos.

As you look at chaos with fresh eyes you'll notice that from a very close perspective there is a marvellous functional structure to it that radiates a wondrous beauty. You will notice when you become more relaxed with ambiguity you will be less inclined to use absolute words like 'never, always, certainly, absolutely' in your conversations. You will notice more carefully the patterns of your own conversations. Do you cut people off before they finish? Are you thinking of what you'll say to them next while they are still talking to you? Do you take a tentative approach or do you tend to be absolutist with your observations? Do you make more statements than ask questions? Do you end your conversations with statements or with curiosity?

You will start to delight in the structures you notice about your own attitude to ambiguity. Ambiguity is the gateway to reasoning critically. Gone is the old idea of chaos. You will feel calm, at ease and curious to discover the unknown. In fact, you will find the ether of uncertainty peculiarly enjoyable!

Paradox

> Good humor is a paradox. The unexpected juxtaposition of
> the reasonable next to the unreasonable.
> —Melvin Helitzer, professor of journalism

One effective, catalytic strategy to promote the value of ambiguity to your colleagues is paradox. A paradox is something that seems ambiguous, absurd and even contradictory, but it is probably true. The word comes from two Greek words, *para* (all around) and *dokein* (to think). This means to think all around, every which way! The purpose of a paradox is to capture attention and provoke fresh thought.

> The point of philosophy is to start with something so simple as not to seem worth stating, and to end with something so paradoxical that no one will believe it.
> —Bertand Russell, philosopher, mathematician and author

Bertrand Russell's paradox is perhaps the most famous of the logical paradoxes. The paradox arises by considering the set of all sets that are not members of themselves. Such a set appears to be a member of itself if and only if it is not a member of itself, hence the paradox. Some sets, such as the set of all teacups, are not members of themselves. Other sets, such as the set of all non-teacups, are members of themselves. Call the set of all sets that are not members of themselves 'S'. If S is a member of itself, then by definition it must not be a member of itself. Similarly, if S is not a member of itself, then by definition it must be a member of itself. Proposed by Bertrand Russell in 1901, the paradox has prompted much work in logic, set theory and the philosophy and foundations of mathematics.

Paradox is a confusion between a frame of reference (a logical level) and the items within that level. For example, consider the liar paradox of, if 'This sentence is not true' is true, then it is not true, and if it is not true, then it is true. Here is a similar example to add clarity. An Italian says, 'All Italians are liars'. This demonstrates how the Italian's self-referential statement oscillates between being a statement and a frame of reference about himself as a statement. The audience is confused about whether, in making the statement, the Italian is lying. If he is lying he is telling the truth. If he is telling the truth he is lying! The Italian's statement can be seen as a frame of reference (logical level) or as an item in that category.

You might like to conclude that to avoid paradox and possible confusion you should ensure expressions do not oscillate between different logical levels. This would mean that an observer of language expressions does not need to choose a logical level to observe from.

However, an observer or participant in a discussion may choose to use the paradox in a creative, poetic or critical way rather than in a confusing way. An observer is always a participant in what is observed and so all statements are statements made by observers because they are participants. Hence all statements (because they are statements by observers) are self-referential and are thus laden with paradox.

Paradox can be used as a tool for distinguishing patterns of communication that underpin human exchanges. The use of logical levels is a tool for observing and creating distinctions and for identifying paradox. The use and appreciation of logical levels is evident in poetry, humour, learning and creativity. Making clear distinctions and confusing distinctions adds to the spice of life and increases our awareness and appreciation of ourselves, the world and the universe (three logical levels!).

Paradox emanates from a flexible mind, from one who is a catalyst. We can see how paradoxes point to different disorderly environments of our century. Here are some examples of paradoxes in play in the business environment and the reasons why they work.

- 'You increase quality by having fewer inspectors, not more.' This indicates that the key to enhancing quality is teamwork, where all members are mutually accountable for producing the synergy evident in quality. All inspection should be self-monitoring and not relying on the 'big stick' of others. Team members need to be involved, to have complementary skills, to be committed to shared goals and to work together. So you might say that you increase quality by becoming your own 'inspector' which reduces the need for inspectors.
- 'You increase competition by increasing cooperation.' To enhance competition it is important to pursue cooperative action with all of one's competitors. This includes partnerships between a company and its suppliers, between a company and its distributors, between management and the workforce and the unions. The secret to increasing competition is greater (not less) cooperation among all sets of necessary partners.
- 'You increase control by relaxing control systems.' Relax bureaucracy. Trust in your talented staff and conduct all customer

service in transparent and ethical ways. These activities require interdependence and delegated cooperation. Emphasise market-driven decision making and fast adaptation by delegating, decentralising and initiating.

- 'You increase stability in a company by promoting change and diversity.' A company's business is to generate strong visions clearly shared and to encourage confident risk-taking and calculated failure so that experimenting and stretching will become useful forces. A company promotes its vision and accepts the events that further refine that vision.

Clearly, the idea of paradox has taught us that if something is contradictory then we know we cannot trust it. So it may be obvious now that when we use paradox we may create mistrust and the urge to examine further. A key to success is the ability to introduce paradox, to deal with it and to reason on all sides. This is what it means to become a critical thinker.

You can also have fun with oxymorons. The word comes from the Greek *oxymoros*, meaning 'sharp' and 'blunt'. In other words, an oxymoron is a seemingly contradictory statement—for example, military intelligence or bitter sweet. You can combine lots of contradictory words such as tight slacks and pretty ugly. Could you put Catholic Christian into this category? Some would say 'no' because they believe Catholicism is a Christian denomination. Others might say 'yes'. For example, they might suggest that who we are is what we believe, and it is impossible for anyone to believe two opposing views simultaneously, because Catholic and Christian are opposing positions.

Here is a list of some oxymorons used in everyday life:

almost certain	cold sweat
almost exactly	common sense
almost never	constant change
among the first	constructive criticism
awfully good	cost effective
bad luck	customer satisfaction
good luck	customer service
clever fool	crash landing

global village
half full
half empty
ill health
inside out
junk food
learning organisation
never again
never mind
new used car
non-stick glue
non-stick gum
non-stop flight
non-working mother
organised chaos
organised confusion

organised crime
organised mess
original copy
perfect idiot
petty cash
politically correct
pot luck
practical experience
public servant
quality service
random patterns
silent alarm
silent scream
thinking critically
true lies
white lies

Word games such as these promote a sense of fun, trust and understanding that might lead the participants to think outside the square, and to increased confidence to suggest different solutions to problems. Think of two contradictory words, an adjective (describing word) and a noun (naming word) or a noun and a verb (doing word) and ask a question about them. For example, take the nouns 'knowledge' and 'management'. Ask, can knowledge be managed? Knowledge management is the explicit and systematic management of vital knowledge and includes creating, gathering, organising and using. It means turning personal knowledge into company knowledge that can be shared and well utilised throughout an organisation. Knowledge is mental and private, while management involves structured process and is public. Some knowledge workers do not like to be managed in the traditional sense. Some might argue that knowledge management is an oxymoron.

You can argue that the phrase 'dual citizenship' is an oxymoron because one cannot truly be a citizen of two different countries because loyalty cannot be divided. Yet those who subscribe to globalisation believe we are citizens of the world, not citizens of a particular country.

Thinking critically is an oxymoron because thinking requires creating patterns and 'critically' means disassembling and re-creating new patterns.

Hobson's choice

The term 'Hobson's choice' is another effective tool for being a catalyst. 'Hobson's choice' probably had its origin in the name of the Englishman Thomas Hobson, born in 1544, 25 years after Leonardo da Vinci died. Hobson kept a livery stable and required every customer to take either the horse nearest the stable door or none at all—that is, they had no choice which horse they could take. In 1914, Henry Ford offered customers of the Model T a famous Hobson's choice, making it available in any colour so long as it was black.

Hobson's choice then is a choice without an alternative; the thing offered or nothing. You can create a Hobson's choice scenario as a dilemma to stir thinking among colleagues. For example, a survey by Jupiter Communications showed that only 6 per cent of e-commerce sales were *new* spending. The rest came out of the hides of brick-and-mortar retailers. They're faced with a Hobson's choice: make the plunge online or face a destructive alternative: gradual extinction. This is provocative, which then leads to further critical reasoning.

If you wish to increase your critical thinking by being a catalyst, you need to create your own paradoxes, ironies and oxymorons. Developing this talent will help to make you an effective explorer of issues and a critical thinker. However, there is one caution you will need to be aware of when you engage in being a catalyst.

If you tell someone they are wrong and you humiliate or belittle them you are not engaging in critical thinking. When you criticise someone it means you are blaming them or condemning them for something they said or did. When you threaten or intimidate some-one you are inflaming their feelings and preventing critical thinking. Harassing someone who is happy with life and forcing them to take a good look at themselves is not helpful to re-examining a situation. This type of response to others does not promote a healthy exploration of the issues. Become a catalyst but do it sensitively, always having respect for others.

Exercise

Welcoming ambiguity

Ambiguity is simply being able to see something in at least two sensible ways, and feeling comfortable in not making sense of a situation. In this exercise all the options indicate a tolerance, acceptance and even a welcoming of ambiguity. Tick the statements that apply to you.

1. I quite like ambiguous situations.
2. I do not find ambiguous situations confusing.
3. Ambiguous situations don't cause me interpersonal problems.
4. I avoid ambiguity in practical situations such as in the need for safety.
5. I create ambiguity when I need to find new ideas.
6. I find it easy to create ambiguity.
7. I think ambiguity is much the same thing as complexity.
8. I search out ambiguity around me a lot.
9. Ambiguity to me is much the same thing as thinking differently.
10. I enjoy reading and creating paradoxes. For example, art is a lie that makes us realise the truth.
11. I entertain ideas that do not have anything to do with the problem at hand.
12. When I find the right answer I look for a second, a third and more right answers.
13. When I figure out what something is, I try and look for another good explanation.
14. I make a point of saying ambiguous things to others.
15. I understand something best when I can see it has many meanings.
16. I interpret my gut feelings in more than one way.

17. I enjoy oxymorons.
18. Bring on contradictions!

What is your score out of 18? The higher the number, the more likely you are to relish the creative potential of ambiguity and being a catalyst.

Become a poet

If thou indeed derive thy light from Heaven,
Then, to the measure of that heaven-born light,
Shine, Poet! in thy place, and be content:
The stars pre-eminent in magnitude,
And they that from the zenith dart their beams,
(Visible though they be to half the earth,
Though half a sphere be conscious of their brightness),
Are yet of no diviner origin,
No purer essence, than the one that burns,
Like an intended watch-fire on the ridge
Of some dark mountain; or than those which seem
Humbly to hang, like twinkling winter lamps,
Among the branches of the leafless trees.
—William Wordsworth, poet

The spin of the hourglass leads us to the poet. To become a poet means to do something different. In order to think critically, we need to think differently. To be different is to assert our uniqueness, to avoid the dangers of groupthink, and to stand out as an individual. Being different challenges basic assumptions.

Why think differently? I have always believed that difference, no matter how small, permeates our existence. We just need to

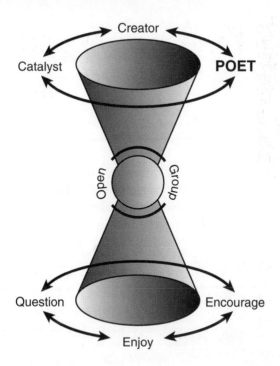

recognise it, enjoy it, imitate it and challenge ourselves. We need to get off the road we usually travel on to change our perspective. Difference brings deeper understanding of the connections in life and of possible new connections that might lead to a greater appreciation and a sense of wellbeing.

One way to start the process of becoming a poet is to use Nature as inspiration. Enjoy a storm, a hot summer's day, a garden, a forest, a desert. Perhaps if you have never done it, go and roll in the grass.

Dare to be different

Poets are people who see things differently and who express things differently. Poets create powerful imagery through juxtaposing particular words in specific ways to make an impact, to give birth to an experience in the reader. There are many poetic devices, such as repetition, rhyme, rhythm, pun, alliteration, onomatopoeia, analogy and metaphor. What better way to illustrate some of these devices than by the last two lines of William Shakespeare's Sonnet 138:

> *Therefore I lie with her, and she with me,*
> *And in our faults by lies we flatter'd be.*

Can you feel the iambic rhythm of one, two, one, two and the rhyming of 'me' and 'be', that is also onomatopoeia because it echoes a soft sound of the meaning? Notice the alliteration (repetition of the soft 'f' consonant sound) in 'faults' and 'flatter'd'. The pun (double meaning) contained in the word 'lie' adds a lovely subtle sense of humour.

Poetry exists in our universe under the rich crimson veil of so many sparkling stars. In nature there flows and erupts such music and dance on the brink of every piercing emotion that ruptures rhythmically through poetic expression. The universe is charged with the grandeur of poetry and everyone who can think critically and creatively can experience and express its wonders. From the moment of our conception we are filled with the poetry of life by feeling the enchanting rhythms and hearing the gurgling rhymes of our mother's magical movements. Poets can transform the ordinary into the extraordinary.

> *Mary, Mary, quite contrary,*
> *How does your garden grow?*
> *'I live with my brat in a high-rise flat,*
> *So how in the world would I know.'*
> —Roald Dahl, author

Being artistic means seeing with different eyes and then expressing what you see in your unique way. Poets challenge routine assumptions. Poets interpret what we take for granted and represent it in a unique way. For example, Salvador Dali sculpted a snail and put wings on it. This is a direct challenge to the basic assumption about a snail's pace. It evokes a personal response because it upsets the taken-for-granted image of a snail. Dali also sculpted and painted human shapes and inserted open empty drawers in their torsos, questioning the assumption about what it means to be a human.

Poets promote difference by taking an existing idea and putting it in a different context or combining two ideas we don't generally associate together, such as the snail with wings. Difference means breaking routine perceptions and patterns. Doing things differently might also mean that we begin to feel in a way we have not recognised before. You might be pro-active in seeking out new ideas, or simply open to them if they happen to come your way. Or you might seek out new ideas with a real zest, but still go on doing the routine things. The idea of difference is a complex one. It can exist in gradations rather than as a dichotomy. For example, only a small part of your experience might be different.

The most exquisite and unprecedented subtleties of life are captured by poets and artists. For poets the eye is the window of the soul. As Leonardo Da Vinci said, 'Who could believe that so small a space could contain the images of the whole universe'. Yes, and who could believe that an equally small space could capture those mellifluous melodies. In fact all of our six senses (sight, sound, smell, touch, taste, intuition), when they so delicately toil together, thoroughly enliven and sustain our spirit. Our brain is much smarter than we think to empower our being in such inventive ways. As we become poets we completely engage in sensory aerobics flaming our discernment and experience. Who better illustrates this than Ogden Nash in a short rhyme on the perfect husband:

He tells you when you've got on too much lipstick
And helps you with your girdle when your hips stick.

Before we look at how to reach the poet within us, let's identify some of the obstacles and inhibitions that may slow us down. These can include timidity, the tyranny of habit, the straitjacket of being an expert and the conventions and rules imposed by society.

Obstacles to being different

Timidity

A husband and wife who travelled from their village in the Middle East to Australia as refugees had never been out of their country before. In fact, they had scarcely left their home town, so the boat trip to Australia was an ordeal and so was being transported from one city to another. No wonder they didn't want to leave the house when they settled in. They didn't want to be taken sightseeing or to the zoo or to the football. Even after many years they preferred to stay at home because that is what they were accustomed to. They only went out to go to work, to walk to their friend's house or to do the shopping.

Their past experience as refugees affected how they now behaved, and this was part of the problem. Their isolated situation eventually made them unhappy. They also had language problems (a familiar obstacle for non-English speaking refugees) that adversely affected their work. They could have had a more satisfying life if they'd felt confident enough to participate in their community. It would have been worth adjusting to their changed circumstances but there were many insurmountable problems for them.

Timidity is distinctive behaviour ingrained from life's experiences, creating a certain level of comfort and safety that becomes a haven from heightened traumatic events. Timidity curtails a richness of experience needed to germinate the poet within us. People will do dramatically different things for survival but may revert to familiar behaviour for comfort where possible.

Habits

A problem with habits is that while they serve us well for survival they are simultaneously insidious. Sometimes we're not even aware we have them. For example, travelling to work might be something we do every day, following the same route. It's easy to take travel for granted, even travel within the city. We are accustomed to moving freely on excursions and visits to friends and other events. We take travel for granted because it becomes a habit. Imagine if you lost all your habits temporarily, your automatic working memory activities disappear and survival is near impossible. It becomes difficult to do several things at once and the drudgery of each day, such as waking, washing, wearing clothes, walking and eating would need to be re-built. We should treasure our habitual brain when it serves us well. Our brains are programmed for survival, which means they are eminently suited to embracing successful modes to make life easier and manageable.

Nearly 30 years ago, Edward de Bono described our brain as a 'self-organising patterning system'. He outlined how the neural networks in the brain that receive information allow the brain to temporarily assemble itself into a succession of steady states. In other words, information impacts on a brain organising itself into patterns, maintaining and building on those patterns! Over time such patterns become habits, preferred perceptual paths and sequences of activity. Our preferences created by our patterns lead us to what we practise, and what we practise is the basis of our proficiency. Expertise then constitutes in great part an easy flow of patterns of behaviour that helps us achieve our intended goal in a field. Our perception translates to our behaviour since our movement is part of our central nervous system. Such an easy flow of predictable patterns of perception and behaviour is what I call habits.

Habits are useful to our survival and functioning because they allow us to recognise things instantaneously and react in terms of previous experience and sequence of activity. Our brain engages in pattern recognition instantaneously and automatically and where the pattern is unrecognisable the brain will match it to the closest pattern that exists in its memory files. Our brain then is a very powerful and efficient self-organising patterning system, like a funnel of pattern recognition.

Habits should not be regarded as fixed all-time solutions to workplace problems. Sticking to certain habits in the workplace is dangerous because the context is constantly changing. The most dangerous type of habit is our interpersonal behaviour. We learn to mould our behaviours to each other according to our personalities and expectations. We learn when to give directions, when to permit others to think aloud, when to question, when to listen, when to share our reactions. We develop theories (practical explanations) of what will work with different people and these become habits of interpersonal operation. We test hunches, intuitions, insights, observations and guesses of what works in different situations with different people. Thus our habits are formed.

Habits are based on good practical theory: we know which assumptions apply to particular situations and why they work, as well as what to do if they don't work. When we use our habits indiscriminately, always automatically, and start to ignore the context and try to fit new situations and surprises into our habitual ways of interacting we give habits an unhealthy dominance, rendering them treacherous. Not only do individuals develop paradoxical habits but so do communities. Sometimes these habits work against thinking critically and thus prevent us becoming a learning community.

Australia is a land of bushfires. Over half a century ago, fierce winds fanned bushfires across Canberra. The catastrophe was tagged 'the powerlines fire' and two people died, over 120 hectares of pine forest were destroyed as well as 13 000 hectares of grassland and bush. Nearly two weeks later, another bushfire destroyed Mt Stromlo observatory buildings with over 320 hectares of pine forest and 3000 hectares of pasture. In the year 2000, during a searing Christmas summer, bushfires caused more havoc and afterwards over half a million pine seedlings were planted in the Mt Stromlo forest to replace the destruction. Then, in January 2003, bushfires raged mercilessly through Canberra again, fanned by winds of up to 100 kilometres per hour. Four people died, over 530 houses were destroyed, Mt Stromlo observatory was obliterated and thousands of hectares of bushland and pine forest razed. Many of those pine trees were planted after previous fires. Our communities seem hardly to have learned anything from half a century of recorded bushfires.

Communities resist change. It is difficult to establish a new life somewhere different after a bushfire. The survivors of the bushfires erect their banners, 'We love our suburb', after its destruction by the fires. We revert to our previous habits. We feel comfortable because of our habits so we cling to what we know and what makes us feel good, our securities. In another half a century when more bushfires hit, we will know if we were able to identify and change our bad habits.

In the late nineteenth century, Samuel Foss wrote 'The Calf-Path'. This poem beautifully illustrates how we adopt each other's thought patterns and habits and over time fail to critically question our assumptions and practice. There is a vicious cycle between habits and mindset. As a result communities fail to learn.

One day, through the primeval wood,
A calf walked home as good calves should;
But made a trail all bent askew,
A crooked trail as all calves do.
Since then two hundred years have fled,
And, I infer, the calf is dead.
But still he left behind his trail,
And thereby hangs my moral tale.
The trail was taken up next day
By a lone dog that passed that way;
And then a wise bell-wether sheep
Pursued the trail o'er vale and steep,
And drew the flock behind him too
As good bell-wethers always do.
And from that day o'er hill and glade,
Through those old woods a path was made.
And thus, before men were aware,
A city's crowded thoroughfare.
And soon, the central street was this,
Of a renowned metropolis.
And men two centuries and a half
Trod in the footsteps of that calf.
Each day a hundred thousand route
Followed this calf about.
And on his crooked journey went
The traffic of a continent.
A hundred thousand men were led
By a calf near three centuries dead.
They followed still his crooked way

And lost one hundred years each day.
For thus such reverence is lent
To well established precedent.

Sticking to our habits means just following our usual ways of doing things. Stable reliable processes are important to any business success and it's important to get basic efficient systems in place, functioning like clockwork. There is a single automatic line of information that says to us that habits are working well and are achieving what the business wants.

Challenging our habits and changing the routines is another way to improve business. When our habits do not produce what they usually do we perceive and experience failure. This second line of information allows us to perceive the situation when the routine breaks down. We have to question and change our habits to anticipate and move forward. Why is this no longer the best way? Why isn't it working as it has before? What are better ways to do this? We question the methods, not necessarily the direction. To get an edge a business should not wait until habits become ineffective but should challenge good habits when they are working well! Rebuild when all is well.

Changing the goals and renewing our vision becomes important in environment that is white water, turbulent and constantly changing. By questioning the direction and the values of the business we can maximize productivity by injecting creativity as a habit! Implement creative inspiration when things are going well.

Any business needs to create different visions of the future. Learning occurs by imagining different futures for the business and by planning for different possible futures. Everyone has creative abilities. It is easy for most adults to think of at least three alternatives for any situation. Children can think of at least 30 options! The longer the list of options the higher the quality of the solution. Search for hidden connections and novel elegant links. Welcome open-ended inquiry and hypothesising! Encourage trial and error and experimentation. Learning comes from thinking freely about your experience. Freedom and a sense of confidence are very important to expanding the capacity of individuals to experiment and to learn from trial and error.

Thinking critically is not a natural talent. Anyone can learn to jolt their own habits, senses and recognition patterns so that what they take for granted becomes a fresh point of focus. All you need is simply a semi-systematic regime of mental exercises to break from your existing mental habits to learn the keys to thinking critically.

Conformity

Australia is in many respects a conventional society. This is portrayed in some of our large institutions. Westpac Bank, Australia's oldest bank with about 200 years of administration was not exactly a model of Australian business success in the 1990s. It had many anachronistic practices. A large number of staff were processing paper and interacting among themselves rather than attending to customers. All of the processing and accounting functions were performed at branch level using swarms of clerks engaged in bookkeeping and ledger work by hand. Huge storage areas were maintained to physically store cheques while awaiting clearance; the branch locations themselves were confined to high streets while much of the population had moved to suburbs and shopped at malls.

Operationally things were just as conservative: transaction standards didn't exist, processing was done manually and products were unresponsive to customer demand. The bank seemed to have an excess of unsuitable staff making bad decisions. The depth and breadth of management experience was lacking as many of them could not enumerate what they had accomplished in those positions; some of this was due to poor recruitment. An orthodox approach to staffing in large organisations is that the human resources departments do the recruiting. A conformist organisation does not allow its managers to hire what they regard as the best talent. Many managers at Westpac with over 25 years' experience had not recruited anyone and therefore had failed to assemble high performing teams to drive superior performance. Problems were left to senior management because of this conformist and follower attitude.

Everything was everyone else's problem and there was no ingrained sense of responsibility or shared accountability.

In Japan there's a saying that 'nails that stick up will be hammered down'. In other words, there's a danger in being different. Certainly, there can be an element of risk involved. Are you strong enough to resist being hammered down? Unless you try it, you'll never know. Become the nail that sticks up. A lot can be learned from challenging assumptions.

Specialisations

We live in an age where job specialisation has grown as a response to the increasing complexity of modern life. Specialisation means an increasing body of knowledge in narrow fields and is one way of increasing the store of knowledge of the human race. Specialisation means that people become highly skilled in particular areas but simultaneously less knowledgeable about broader areas. You visit the doctor because you do not feel well and he or she will refer you on to a specialist if they cannot deal with the issue. A mechanic will refer you on to a specialist if the garage doesn't have the equipment to diagnose the smart chip in your car. Increasingly, people respond to a problem by saying that they can't deal with it because it is not in their area of expertise. Sometimes the response 'that's not my area' is an excuse for poor customer service.

Many of us are familiar with the experience of ringing an organisation with a problem and being put on a merry-go-round of different departments. Added to this problem is the fact that people in related specialisations find it increasingly difficult to communicate with each other. A psychologist looks at people as a set of personality characteristics while a social worker sees them as members of a group. Each specialisation has its own unique perspective, which is essential, but can lead to the trap of only considering one aspect of an issue. In medicine, for example, the general practitioner sees people as complex integrated systems, the orthopaedic surgeon looks at us as bags of bones, the cardiologist focuses on the mechanism of the heart, the gastroenterologist sees the body as a digestive and elimination system and so on.

The Roman poet Virgil once said, 'Follow an expert'. My exhortation is to engage in multitudinous expertise to 'question all experts'. Becoming a poet is a way of engaging in different perspectives, of keeping the whole in mind, of not falling into the specialisation trap. Thinking critically beckons us to engage in many specialisations. In the workplace the practice of multi-skilling, itself a result of thinking critically, is introduced to counteract the weary effects of specialisation.

Rules and conventions

Cultural blocks can limit thinking critically. The expectations that others place upon us, the rules of our particular society and the structures of our institutions, businesses, education and social systems act as inhibitors to people thinking for themselves. People who break cultural rules tend to be seen as negative and destroyers of the status quo. Often it happens subtly because people are discouraged from considering alternatives that might be viewed as inappropriate by the cultural and social standards, and inconsistent with the prevailing norms and the rules of the game.

People are known to carry out their jobs with such precision and scrupulousness that borders on an unhealthy practice of inflicting pain and harm on others unnecessarily. There appears to be a deep-seated sense of adherence to duty, rules and conventions in human beings, especially when it is required through the directions issued by superiors and authority figures. It is not so much that the detailed rules and conventions exist, rather that authorities command their strict adherence which creates a climate that discourages people from thinking critically. Institutions and organisations establish systems that constrain actions through pressure to conform. People follow orders that result from policies even when those orders lead to death. The 1960s war in Vietnam and the movement of troops and war on Iraq in recent times are two examples of extracting high levels of solidarity to rules and conventions of authority.

Of course, these patterns are established from birth when children are trained to obey their parents and other legitimate authority.

Teachers command children. Even though corporal punishment is illegal in Australian schools, substitute sanctions carry the same effects. There were famous experiments performed at Yale University where a large number of graduate psychology students were asked to estimate how many people would administer a 450-volt shock to another person. They predicted a low 1 to 2 per cent. About 40 psychiatrists predicted only 0.001 per cent would administer that level of shock. The psychology professor, Stanley Milgram, then asked volunteers to role-play a teacher and to deliver increasingly intensive and dangerous levels of shock to learners when they gave the wrong answers (even if they started kicking and pleading). The volunteers did not know the learners (the victims) were actors who pretended to be shocked by the shocks administered by them on demand. Milgram was interested to discover just how much suffering an ordinary person will inflict on an innocent person because they are following the rules from authority, when it is their job. To everyone's amazement, over 60 per cent of the volunteer teachers gave every level of the 30 shocks on command, to the maximum 450 volts!

Rules and conventions have an unhealthy aspect of creating a climate of not thinking. We have seen peaceful protesters run over by tanks as a result of soldiers following the rules of command. People may hate what they are doing but they still follow the rules of authority. Historically, the religious possessed the knowledge and power of authority. Today that has been weakened. The medical profession and scientists still hold much power and influence and when they make clear errors it is unlikely that others of lower rank will question them. In issuing medication alone, some hospitals record anything up to a 15 per cent daily error rate. Up to 10 per cent of all cardiac arrests have been attributed to errors in medication. A lot of this is because of a mindless deference given to the person in charge, the expert who supposedly knows the rules of the game better than anyone else. Many medical personnel do not explain to their patients the nature of their complaint nor the nature of the intervention and the patients themselves are discouraged from asking. An important duty of the experts, professionals, leaders, managers and people in authority is to encourage others to use their initiative through challenging rules and conventions—through thinking critically.

Solutions to obstacles

Do nothing

A prerequisite to doing something different is freeing ourselves from some of our habits. Just doing nothing is a good way to begin. This may seem like a silly exercise—perhaps you feel you're good at doing nothing already!—but some people find it almost impossible to do nothing. It can be quite hard to achieve. If you work in an unfriendly environment or you feel stressed by colleagues, friends or family or have too many demands on your time, you may find it difficult to create time for yourself.

Compulsive activity can also be a habit. Most of us do not like to waste time but some people, who are 'workaholics', really dread the idea of wasting a single moment. Even spending time on frivolous and fun-filled activities is time well spent. Doing nothing means putting yourself in a full state of peace of mind. Readying yourself to be poetic. Becoming relaxed. Sitting quietly and breathing slowly. As Emile Coué said, 'Every day in every way, I'm getting better'. We could change this to 'Every day in every way, I'm getting more poetic'.

I think I am poetic, therefore I am poetic. We are what we think. Quiet time is good for reflection. Think of situations you might be in and see if you can plan a poetic response. Learn from others. For example, rock musician Frank Zappa was once asked, 'I guess your long hair makes you a girl?' His response was, 'I guess your wooden leg makes you a table.' This is bordering on poetic as it provides unique imagery and stirs the being. The juxtaposition is surprising with an injection of light humour—notice the double use of the word 'makes'. I think that qualifies as poetic!

Do different things

The key to doing something differently is finding something different to do. Sounds simple enough, doesn't it, but how many people relish this idea and how many would prefer to go on doing what they've always done?

Doing something different means adapting an existing action from one situation to another. You do not need to make a fantastic discovery, you just need to do it. So, if you haven't done it before, experience a magic show and decide to really enjoy it. Get soaking wet in the rain. Go see a comedy play and laugh—a hearty, belly laugh. Experience what you are unaccustomed to. You might even take up a new hobby such as acting. Do something different and notice how you start to think differently. Change does not work in only one direction and you don't have to think of something different before you do it. Go to a new place and engage. Allow the doing to fold back on your thinking.

Play the fool

In a circus, the fool plays the role of presenting the absurd to us. Fools create humour by ridiculing what we hold as true. We may laugh when we see a person sitting backwards on a merry-go-round horse, but from the fool's point of view the horse is facing the wrong way. Fools are blind to problems others see as obvious, yet fools see things others overlook. Their irreverence raises our awareness of assumptions because they reverse what we take for granted.

Being a fool is a form of thinking critically. Thinking critically is the blatant pursuit of diversity for diversity's sake. Reach for a sweeping spectrum of perspectives. You can't do this easily or comprehensively if you stick to the rules. Tom Peters, the management guru, says, 'Rules are for fools'. Of course, in this book I am encouraging you to be a fool as well, so I believe this does not mean to completely abandon rules—play the fool with them and avoid unnecessary and inhibiting constraints. This requires judgement. Poets break rules for the heck of it as well as just to experiment and capture the freshness.

If you're ready to risk looking foolish for the cause of poetry, you'll need to identify some of the things you generally avoid, precisely in order not to appear silly. These might include:

- challenging what others say
- making serious statements and then contradicting yourself
- asking silly questions: for example, the meaning of basic objects
- rigorously defending points of view you disagree with.

Doing these things might help you to identify what you do believe in, or see others' points of view.

When you allow yourself to be foolish and laugh at yourself it may release a sense of creativity and fun that is infectious. Others will get the idea you are fooling around and support your attempts to be creative. It is amazing how even odd behaviour can be catchy and you will always find some people who will take an interest. You can easily find something different to do to go against the flow of mainstream behaviour and incite action in others.

We want to be different to be unique but our similarities in purpose and in action are what bind us and give us our identity. Consider a woman who boards a bus to go to work, looks around and realises everyone is wearing a party hat and holding a balloon. The woman accepts a hat and balloon from the driver and is caught up with the flow of the action in much the same way that a person driving on a busy highway is forced to drive at the same speed as the vehicles around him. The flow of the traffic and the flow of the mood on the bus are like waves pushing people into the action flow. Part of being human means being gregarious and going with the flow. Humans model behaviour as a support and comfort in life. Being a poet means inspiring others to do different things.

Learn to do what you want to do

Planning may not seem like poetry, but identifying what you want to do is a basic part of self-expression. Your unique characteristics need to be given space to breathe. Of course, there are constraints on all of us. We have commitments. We want and need some of those commitments and cannot imagine ourselves without them.

But are we doing what we want to do or did we fall into our life, having never revised our ideas? Being poetic requires a disposition of choice and freedom. Whether or not others expect us to do things is not the issue.

We can fill our free time with things we really want to do. We can find ways to increase or reduce time where we really can choose what we do.

Meddling, muddling and modelling

When you are bored, lost or just looking for something to do it isn't too difficult to start meddling in other people's activities to create some hype for yourself. When your job has lost its zest and challenge of course you'll be prone to interfering with others' work. You need to review you current situation. Did you choose your current job and lifestyle? Are you happy with them? Or do you feel you are just muddling along, that you are trapped? Maybe your dissatisfaction is more vague. Do you feel unhappy in a general way about your present situation? Are you just coasting along without being really engaged in anything? Now is the time to take stock and think about how you really want to spend the rest of your life.

Create a model of what you really want to be doing. Make a list of all the things you have always wanted to do. Recall your childhood dreams: What did you want to be as an adult? What things in life have come easily to you? What things would you like to come easily to you? Imagine there were no constraints on you: What sort of life would you want to pursue? Now, will you just continue muddling along or will you decide to choose to do something different? Who will you model yourself on—someone you know or the person you really want to be?

Being poetic means expressing yourself in the way you want to live your life. Choose what you want and play with what you can't have to create new perspectives.

Use language

I'm not suggesting you abandon your career to become a poet. Rather, the idea is to try and use some of the *poetic tools* to assist your capacity for critical thought. By taking a leaf out of the poet's book, you can use devices such as analogy, metaphor, paradox, irony, oxymoron, hyperbole, rhyme and rhythm to help you to think differently. And by borrowing from a clown's repertoire, you can learn to stand assumptions on their heads. It is not a simple matter of making a fool of ourselves. Nor is it a simple matter of realising that we have fixed patterns of thinking. But both of these things help.

Words can have powerful connotations over and above their definition in the dictionary. For example, the terms 'intellectual capital' or 'human capital' are recent examples of modern managerialism. Most people in the industry click with these terms immediately but for others they will be seen as demeaning of the human spirit. The words 'intellectual' and 'human' are the subordinate adjectives and it may be seen as insulting to juxtapose them with the noun 'capital'. In this way, the same word will be a 'snarl' word to some while being a 'purr' word to others. Take the word 'sorry', for example. How do you feel about this word? Do you like it, detest it or are you nonchalant about it? The word means 'regret' but in Australia at the moment there are layers of emotions attached to this word. Some see it as a synonym for reconciliation between the descendants of those people who arrived after 1788 and the indigenous population. Media coverage of the issue has highlighted the fact that Prime Minister John Howard has been careful not to use the word when discussing indigenous affairs. Others have felt equally strongly that an apology *is* necessary. The power of the word was evident in the year 2000 when it was unfurled on banners and slowly inscribed in smoke by a tiny silver aeroplane circling above the marchers for reconciliation over the Sydney Harbour Bridge.

Of course, not everyone feels the same about this or any other particular issue. Your emotions will differ according to your own history and experience. So, when it comes to language, it's important to be aware that words can carry at least two levels of meaning— the definition and the feelings that individual people have about it based on their personal experiences.

There are, however, potentially an infinite number of other perceived levels of meanings in words. These levels might be random

—for example, parallel, exact, diffuse, humorous etc.—or they might be dichotomous, conceived as open-ended continuums—such as soft–hard, masculine–feminine, single–multiple, forward–backward, vertical–horizontal etc. Others include:

- negative or positive, for example, a string of words that might form a continuum—murder, kill, put down, pass away, reborn—that can be seen as either negative or positive
- active or passive—force, command, persuade, negotiate, discuss, listen, submit
- powerful or weak—red, orange, yellow, green, blue, white, black, grey.

The weight of the meanings of these can depend on personal responses. For example, some people prefer to use the word 'woman' when describing a female, rather than 'lady' as 'lady' has sexist connotations, while 'woman' can be regarded as neither good nor bad but quite an active, strong word. Conversely, some people might take exception to being referred to as a woman, rather than a lady, which suggests they believe 'woman' is a negative description. But not all words need be put into the 'snarl' and 'purr' categories. You can feel neutral about words as well, and 'woman' might be a neutral word for you.

The delights of thinking critically is that every view conceivable potentially exists in reality; we just need to recognise where it does occur even if it is in the imagination. Reasoning is the mechanism that keeps the status quo and surprisingly it divides more than unites. Reasoning critically opens up many options and can potentially unite minds on all fronts. The poetic device of hyperbole can be used as a jolt. When you exaggerate purposely people will take notice and thus you create an opportunity to explore differences. Critical thinkers appreciate they have never understood the infinite number of perspectives there are to comprehend any situation. They challenge this by stretching the use of language—thinking about the use of categories, analogies, similarities and differences and metaphors to do so.

Question categories

Learning to think differently requires us to avoid futile or faulty generalisations. A generalisation is an attempt to make comparisons and contrasts by classifying things and sorting them into groups on the basis of accepted categories. We all tend to group items on the basis of their similarities and their differences.

When you have 'good' experiences you feel good and tend to see the world around you as good. Similarly, when you have 'bad' experiences you feel bad and tend to see the world around you as bad. Our immediate experiences and our egocentric tendencies combine to produce a distorted generalisation about the reality surrounding us. When we fail to adopt a 'long view' we allow current emotional reactions to influence our generalisations about events around us. This may lead to mistaken persistent attitudes ranging from a sweeping cynicism to a silly exuberance.

In difficult situations we tend to generalise when there are pressures and we need to find a cause or put blame somewhere. Common targets of blame are the government or 'the system' or our boss or someone else who prevents us from doing what we want to. In reality, there are many systems that deserve some measure of blame—bureaucracy, sexism and discrimination of other types— but it is unproductive to passively categorise events on this basis. It is more useful to trace the generalisation to the problem and try to tackle the underlying issues by taking responsibility and clarifying the values underpinning your position.

To understand this, consider what it would mean if you categorised a restaurant as either creative or logical. Logical might mean you take a functionalist approach, ensuring customers have quick and easy service and are served the basics, a good hearty meal. Creative might mean you aim to give a full 'dining' experience that is memorable—people would need time to savour the delicacies and would know they should not just come in for a quick snack. Your concept would attract a certain clientele. The concept of finance, likewise, if put in a creative category would point to 'creative' accounting and in a logical category might mean a focus on just the basics without the fancy manoeuvres.

Try putting these words into the two categories of creative and logical to see how you think upon the words and the categories.

finance	return on investment	work plans
sport	bridge	holidays
staff training	investment	story
service	restaurant	ship
audit	management	leadership
hobbies	singing	opera
customers	timetable	space
pay	appraisal	universe

You could probably categorise any words quite easily in many different ways—for example, those things easy to count and those not easy to count, or things we like and those we dislike. The danger is that we tend to simplify life into the good and the bad, the 'is' and the 'isn't'. Generally speaking, life does not fall into two neat categories even though we can find powerful examples of where it does. The mind abhors chaos and we like to see patterns in everything even when there is no pattern intended. Only if we cannot discern a pattern do we then reluctantly admit that it does not make sense to us. So to think critically as a poet one needs to question the categories we place things in.

Analogy

The essence of analogy is that you try to make connections between two dissimilar things. Analogy works on the principle of association. You begin from what you know and go to an unknown object or idea by linking one or more elements. Analogy is a good source of thinking differently and a key skill for becoming a poet.

A generalisation is a comparison based on accepted categories— for example, fair-skinned people burn more easily in the hot sun than dark-skinned people. An analogy is also a comparison, but of two things we choose regardless of their acceptability—for example, you are lovely like a summer's day, or you run like a stilted pelican labouring to lift off the ground. For this reason analogy is potentially poetic.

To compare two things is to say how they are the same in at least one way. We might compare the way certain things function such as a hand is like a shovel. Here, the common function of the scooping movement is the similarity. Another hand movement example is: The bricklayer's large lean hands laboured more delicately than those of a temple dancer. Or we might say, the earth is like a ball, referring to its shape. Her face is as red as a sunset, where colour is the comparative category. He is heartless and cold as marble—emotion and the kinaesthetic are the focus of the comparison here.

The purpose of using analogy is clear in the above examples. Analogies provide a vivid and clear explanation because putting them together creates a lucid association that might provoke a different way of feeling and thinking about them. We can also use analogies to provide greater clarity and appreciation of complex concepts or unfamiliar things because they compare something we are very familiar with and something we may not be very familiar with. For example, a carburettor works on air-flow just like the strong air-flow over an aeroplane's wings that keeps the plane airborne.

The great advantage of analogies is the vivid imagery they create. A few basic things in our world, such as life and family, can show how we randomly create analogies. In fact, we can use the same analogies with each.

1. Life is like:
   - a banana—you start small and green, become firm and go mushy when old.
   - cooking—you can choose the ingredients and cook them in your own way.
   - a maze—you get pushed into it, you can easily get lost and disoriented but you try to enjoy the journey.
   - a puppy—playful, unruly, excited.
   - a lift—you constantly go up and down, you might get stuck if you're not careful, but worst of all, you dislike it when things don't go smoothly.

2. The family is like:
   - a banana—the outer skin protects the young fruit until it's

ready to be peeled away to expose the mature fruit to the world.

- cooking—members (ingredients) need to mix well in order to live together/interact to make the family (the recipe) work.
- a maze—you can journey together but usually exit alone.
- a puppy—some members always are looking for food and play while others are trying to please them.
- a lift—members sometimes travel together but also go up and down at different times.

See if you can think up random analogies for work using the above words—banana, cooking, maze, puppy and lift.

Metaphor

A metaphor is like an analogy but it links two particular things by ascribing the characteristics of one thing to another quite different thing. An example of an analogy would be: time is like a gently flowing river. A metaphor would be: time flows.

Metaphors are powerful because they contain action. A metaphor helps us to understand an idea through the power of its vivid action. Here is a list of vivid action words followed by an unexpected or stark connection. Think about what gives each metaphor its power.

- caressing talent
- stitching ideas
- riding your dreams
- amalgamating stains
- bicycling through the joys of life
- hammering the candle wick
- haring down the river
- extinguishing services.

Each metaphor has a noun and a verb: talent is caressed; ideas are stitched; dreams are ridden; stains are amalgamated; you bicycle through life, the wick is hammered and you extinguish in service.

* * *

Poetry is about imagery, sound and movement: the eyes, ears and central nervous system. Everyone can become a poet! We all have the poet within us. Simply ask yourself this series of questions:

• What is the image I have now and what is another image I can create?
• What sound patterns do I hear now and what other sounds can I create?
• What movement do I feel and what other movement can I create?

To become a poet there are two simple steps. First, you challenge what you are focusing on—tug it, tease it, turn it, twist it, tighten it, detach it, set it free. Thinking critically means challenging by asking about it, reversing assumptions and exaggerating or distorting them in some way. Second, you create new imagery, sound and movement. Becoming a poet means moving out of the ordinary experience and creating new imagery, sounds and movement to startle, inspire and to shake your central nervous system with stimuli of all sorts.

> Paradoxically though it may seem, it is none the less true that
> life imitates art far more than art imitates life.
> —Oscar Wilde, dramatist

Exercise

Similarities and differences

It will be useful to sharpen your thinking by practising to discern attributes among two seemingly unrelated things or ideas. Identify at least three similarities shared by each pair of items below and at least one point of difference between them.

• a fish and a bird
• a family and a globe

- a leaf and a house
- a ball and a dodecahedron (a twelve-sided object)
- the numbers 5 and 89.

Identify at least three differences shared by each pair of items below and at least one point of similarity between them.

- freedom and authority
- mathematics and technology
- the Internet and a spider's web
- thinking and dreaming
- the numbers 6 and 90.

Become a creator

Hell, there are no rules here—we're trying to accomplish something.
—Thomas Edison, inventor and physicist

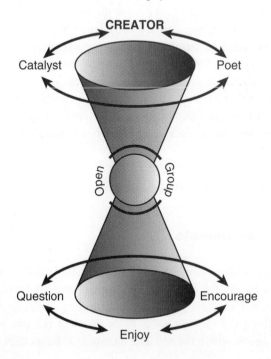

What are the rules we live by right now? What are the ethics that govern the way we make a living? We are in a creative phase of development in our attitude towards work. Many more people now than last century want balance in their life but they also want the workplace to be flexible, liberating, creative and enjoyable. Have we entered the Creative Century because of the way so many people want to, and should work? We need to become creators of different rules if we value our democratic and diverse environments.

Customer service is a twenty-first century creative hype. The creativity of this focus is seen in the novel practices and vision statements supporting businesses who want to be employer of choice, to exceed customer expectations, to cooperate. For example, the Australian Federal Police have a new motto: To fight crime together and win. The University of Canberra's logo is: The University for Creative Professionals. So changes are being seen.

Talent-focus is another recent creative business approach. Many companies who want the best talent have discovered inventive ways of poaching the best people globally. The metaphor used for this approach is unfortunately 'the talent war'. There are all sorts of incentives used to capture the best employees and a key one is providing a work environment to collaborate with dynamic, friendly, creative and challenging staff. Thinking critically is a positive creative force that uses explicit challenges to energise life and business. When you put people first, the business takes on a creative shape compared to the lack of creativity that results when people are not valued.

In order to create different rules we need to understand how people and business operate.

How people operate

I would like to share some lessons I learned while strolling along the Rambla in Barcelona. Since the Olympic Games in 1992, tourists flock in greater numbers than before to the city and delight in promenading along the famous walk. At one end of the one-kilometre route is a beach where the red and blue tourist buses depart and at the other end is the famous square of Cataluyna with its sparkling fountains and flocks of pigeons. The question I reflected on is the way in which different rules for making a living are created by beggars, cowboys, scoundrels and clowns.

The beggar

You will see beggars on the corners of many streets in Barcelona, especially near the traffic lights where they can catch the converging crowds as they cross the road. One beggar I observed was a fully clad woman, face well hidden behind a black shawl, stooped as if she had scoliosis, quivering as she slowly manoeuvred to and fro, turning this way and that to catch the crowds but never making eye contact. She was a picture of extreme suffering and depravation. In one hand she held out a wooden bowl to ask for donations and in the other a walking stick, her only support.

While I watched her for ten minutes, three people took pity on her and threw a small coin into her bowl. Then she lurched across an intersection to the opposite corner of the square and repeated her actions, but the hit rate of donations remained low, perhaps one in every three to five minutes. Her behaviour was persistent and she had some skill in appealing to the crowd's sense of kindness and pity, yet it was obvious that her pathetic aura disgusted many passers-by.

Some executives are like this, forever chasing favours, seeking partners and accepting sponsors and donations to make themselves popular, but at what cost? Some employees have similar qualities to the beggar using all their talent un-creatively and passively—on a quest for crumbs.

The entertainer

> Imagination rules the world.
> —Napoleon Bonaparte, Emperor of France

A hundred metres away from the beggar was a man dressed like the cowboy John Wayne, all painted in gold, one hand on his gun and the other relaxed against his hip. He stood on a golden suitcase, motionless and more graceful than Michelangelo's statue of David. In front of the case was a golden-coloured teapot for accepting coins. People stopped to stare just as they had at the beggar, but this time it was in awe, not pity. What skill he possessed to remain completely inert!

Clank! A small child dropped a gold coin into the teapot. The statue came to life. A golden thumb was retrieved from the fist clenched around the gun, the elbow was straightened and the famous gesture, the thumbs-up, brought a smile to the crowd that was gathering. The eyes gleamed with life and one winked three or four times as the white teeth peeped from behind the golden lips parting in a beam of euphoria. The eye contact was tremendously rewarding. Someone else threw another gold coin and again there was the magic of the novel thumbs-up gesture, the winks and the beaming greeting. Now a young woman daintily donated a coin and the cowboy went through his routine again with creative variation, making it seem as fresh as the first time. You could not tire of admiring him.

Some executives are like this, striding the stage of their corporations like a colossus. They have the command and opportunity through their image and body language to lift the spirit of the organisation and create positive hype and joy in the business. Yet, some are superficial in this approach and simply want to be admired by their staff, in return rewarding only those who oblige and give their attention. A pity that, like the cowboy, some executives tend to ignore and abandon many of the frontline staff who do not pay homage to them, those who do the majority of the frontline work.

The scoundrel

> If you obey all the rules, you miss all the fun.
> —Katharine Hepburn, actor

There are many teams working in and around the square whose aim is to cheat unsuspecting tourists of their money. I saw one team composed of five men in action. They each cooperate to extract a 5000-peseta note ($50) from their victim. The performance involves a cardboard box folded into a mobile table, a tiny red pea and three caps, made from the ends of hollowed-out carrots. The game requires you to guess under which cap the red pea is to win 5000 pesetas. If you're wrong, you lose the 5000 pesetas.

The team only stays in the one place for a short while and then shuffles along, just in case anyone becomes wise to their game. The master player juggles the pea under each cap and tries to confuse the onlookers as to where it lands. To begin with, the players are often his own team members who win and lose convincingly in order to attract real players. The team plays the crowd, cajoling people to earn some easy money. They use their bodies to block the view, they push and nudge onlookers, creating a sense of confusion and they even point out the cheating so as to pretend to be honest witnesses. When one unsuspecting tourist guessed where the pea was he was distracted for only 30 seconds, by which time the position had been furtively changed and his correct observation turned out to be wrong. He lost his money!

It was difficult to determine the rate of return, but I suspect with five in the team the business had to be lucrative! These scoundrels had created an entertainment business based on dishonesty and deception.

Some executives shuffle the furniture, refurbish and with the team attract new clients just like a team of con-artists. They seem to be successful but unless they act ethically and in the best interests of customers they find they soon have to shuffle along in case anyone wises up to their game. Unethical behaviour is based on a lack of learning and the wrong ordering of priorities, which eventually leads to failure. There is no better example to illustrate this than Australia's corporate collapses during the 1980s, the biggest string of corporate disasters in the country's history. Some of Australia's past heroes ended up looking like fools because of their inability to learn from their mistakes.

Success is no proof of virtue and virtue is not a guarantee of success either. No single factor can guarantee success but learning, more than any other factor, leads to success. Small businesses in

Australia are notoriously vulnerable to economic and political factors and the bulk of Australian small businesses fail. Large businesses are harder to slay—destruction is usually achieved through incompetent management that consists of a failure to develop and learn. Failure is also due to a singular self-interest, call it greed, and unreasonable arrogance as witnessed in the nomadic confidence tricksters. The collapses in the 1980s in Australia were due to this sort of attitude. The words of the Australian journalist and author, Trevor Sykes, are very telling about the failure caused by a lack of learning.

> If engineers never learned from history every generation of students would be condemned to reinvent the wheel. But engineers and scientists do learn from history, and so we have seen heart transplants and human beings walking on the moon. In economics and finance, however, the human race still starts every generation with flint axes.
> —Trevor Sykes, author and journalist

A paradox is that failure can be as valuable as success due to its learning properties. A goal for everyone then is to hurry up and get failure out of the way so they can start succeeding. Thomas Watson, the founder of IBM said that if we want to be successful faster, then we should double our rate of failure!

The clown

Another significant experience I had on the Rambla was meeting the most beautiful clown I have ever seen. I was immobilised by his superb paraphernalia, flamboyant colours and his huge grin. What was unusual about this street performer was that he had divided his body into two parts. The left half was dressed to symbolise modern life with its stresses and bright technological colours while the right half was a reminder of the trappings of the past with conservative earthy colours and black and white. His face was painted to match the binary system of his costume. In his left hand he held a slim case, perhaps a laptop computer. In his right hand was a wad of tiny folded pieces of coloured paper. He achieved a strong luring effect through his dress, body paint, postures, colours and the concepts he portrayed. He was the yin and the yang, two versions of a story, two clowns in one, the right half of the brain and the left side simultaneously exposed. To gaze at him was to be rewarded twice!

The clown's unifying feature was the glorious expression on his visage. *Thud!* Coins landed in the softly padded base of his beautifully adorned velvet urn. In an instant the clown performed a wonderful jig. Then he leaned over and quietly uttered these words to me: 'Spanish, English, French or German?' I replied, 'English', and he gave me a pink piece of paper from his right hand. Saying, 'Thank you', he returned to his previous posture. Again, I gazed in awe and then as I strolled along I unfolded the tiny piece of paper and read his message.

Here's a little secret: the *left* side of your body is connected with your dreams. So if you want to remember your dreams and better understand them, you've got to learn to do things with your left hand, like writing, combing, shaving, smoking, kicking or throwing a ball. The *right* side of your body (your right hand) has to learn the subtle art of backing up the actions of your left hand. These reversed actions will amplify your sensibility and enhance your health, as well as expand your consciousness and creativity. You don't need to change any of your habits or customs. Just change hands. The same applies to your arms, legs and feet. (All is reversed if you are a left-hander.) In these hard times, spiritual growth can come now *only* through your left side, your female aspect (if you are a man) or your male aspect (if you are a woman). Do it yourself and teach and help your kids to master both their sides while they are growing. This will make them stronger, healthier and . . . happier!

Some executives are like the clown, always trying to energise their staff, eager to share their vision and to achieve business enlightenment in a joyful way.

Of all these people working the streets of Barcelona, which type would you aspire to emulate? Do you admire the beggar who was marketing pity? Do you admire the cowboy who promoted friendship? Perhaps you admire the scoundrels who were the epitome of cunning? How easy do you think it might be to emulate the effer-vescent clown offering joy and enlightenment? They all were an expression of their imagination—even the beggar had the courage to find perhaps the only means of survival imaginable, just as the scoundrels injected their imagination into their cunning.

We might prefer to say they marginalised rather than flowered their imagination. Imagination is inclusive of justification and all of our powers and proclivities to progress, while at the same time inconclusive and indiscriminate—all the reasons and yet none of them specifically qualify when you are imagining. First you imag-ine, then the reason might reveal itself and years later others will find more reasons. Yet it is possible to harness this extraordinary power. We need an inner freedom to unleash our imagination beyond our location in life. Life is not without its measures. We use our experiences as measures and we express these as comparisons and contrasts. We notice different people around us behaving like all of these Spanish characters, energised by their imaginations, working their imaginings to the limits of their own mental liberty. This is what adds to the spice of life and gives us a reservoir of valu-able experience as the basis for thinking critically. *La vita é bella.*

I reflected on how these people achieved their results. Imagin-ation is the most powerful tool of progress. The cowboy didn't look like a beggar, although the end result—money given by the public—was the same. Yet what a difference there was between the two performers. One was a reminder of misery, abandonment and abject poverty. The other was an example of entrepreneurship, hope, ingenuity and wealth. Here were two mindsets that created two opposing strategies to achieve the same ends. As you might expect, the cowboy was far more successful financially, appealing to people's sense of awe, beauty and intrigue. The entertainer repre-sents our happy spirit, the joyful workplace giving the thumbs-up to the pursuit of cheerful participation, genuine cooperation and a truly democratic workplace. The clown represents the full form of unleashed imagination, creativity and the life balance we value in the third millennium.

There might be a training course in the making for teaching entrepreneurial skills to beggars, but it wouldn't attract any clients or an income! The beggar is an apt metaphor for those in our organisations that do not value learning. An unwillingness to learn is a formidable challenge to progress. The cowboys and entertainers would relish extending their repertoire of already successful skills. The team of scoundrels is quite a different consideration. Its members used skill, cooperation and effective teamwork. Ethics training for this group of scoundrels is a strategy that is sure to fail on three counts—they wouldn't attend the training, they wouldn't pay the fees and they wouldn't change their ways. Nor again would the beggar or the artist change their ways. But, to be a clown—ahh!—so scintillating and joyful, making life worth living and work worth labouring.

Life on the Rambla is a rich tapestry of what it means to be human and life inside organisations can be just as varied and unpredictable. In a knowledge economy, all are using knowledge to the same ends. But we should consider if we truly imagine in a ferocious and free way. Imagining is a form of thinking critically without the thinking but by picturing. You don't need to visit Barcelona to find this out.

Better ways for companies to operate

> In the beginning the Universe was created. This has made a lot
> of people very angry and has been widely regarded as a bad
> move.
> —Douglas Adams, author

Organisations establish controls so they can compete and win. They create processes and rules, shape roles for workers, set boundaries, establish strategies and reward conformist behaviour. A highly competitive company is one that breeds conformity to its controls.

In most cases competition has become a game of hopping on the same bandwagon. One firm lowers its prices and the others follow. One company gives greater benefits to its customers—for example, three-year guarantees—and the others will soon follow the same strategy. Highly competitive companies may offer even greater rewards, perhaps four- or five-year guarantees. One airline introduces a reward program with frequent flyer points and the other airlines follow to lure back any lost customers. Industries copy competitive strategies from other industries. It seems everyone follows the same rules once they are established.

Being competitive by following the rules—focusing on quantity, costs and quality—is a conformist strategy that seems impossible to avoid. Here, measurement and achieving the bottom line are seen as all-important. Is it possible to break the rules and still be competitive? Many organisations are seeking to break away from this old mind-set. In order to do this, they would need a new organisational model.

Some believe that people are the primary asset of the organ-isation. At least this is the rhetoric. People are to be valued, encouraged to contribute and shown appreciation for their efforts. But how will valuing people as assets work competitively? Do companies value their own people or others, the 'supposed' best in the field?

The word benchmark, used in surveying, refers to the stake in the ground that acts as a reference point for other measurements. Fifteen years ago, business borrowed this term and uses it as a band-wagon to find out *how* other people do things. But benchmarking other people identifies many benchmarks and still leaves the ques-tion, of which stake shall we take notice. Which do we implement? Management by imitation is not a way to value one's own talent but creates ambiguities about how they 'really' did it.

You have to do it for yourself. You have to have full confidence of uncertainty and the freedom and courage to truly value your talent—implement, try it, fail it, re-build it. It's simple enough: value people first and back them with the required resources for successful implementation. Most failures are failures in implemen-tation, not failures in planning. I will give some suggestions on how to make it a reality.

A new paradigm

I think computer viruses should count as life. I think it says something about human nature that the only form of life we

have created so far is purely destructive. We've created life in
our own image.
—Stephen Hawking, theoretical physicist

We live in a tolerant society and as long as we do not cause harm to others it is possible to implement change if we can demonstrate its benefits. An open-minded culture is the right environment for breaking the rules, so approach your concerns with confidence. Exercise your freedom, your confidence and your capacity to tolerate and welcome the uncertainty that change may bring.

If you look on your company as a part of society, you may feel that organisations have a duty to contribute to society as well as to attend to their own survival and prosperity. According to this point of view, staff should be allowed to feel they are contributing to society and not solely to increasing the company's profits. Mutual support in aspirations between individuals and the group tends to enhance goal achievement of all parties. For the company it might mean a better social profile because it is acting in socially responsible ways, and for individuals it would mean greater satisfaction and happiness about working for a company with a social conscience. Where there are areas of common interests between individuals and the institution, both will prosper.

The tip of an iceberg represents about one-ninth of its total size. Think of your business as an iceberg. The visible tip represents the physical and financial resources of your company while the hidden bulk underneath represents the intellectual capital of your staff. That's why it's worth valuing your human resources.

Here are a few things you could do to change your company's traditional culture:

- Change the executive structure from a top-down control to a bottom-up empowerment. This gives every person the opportunity to influence and to break the rules.
- Have fewer management structures to ensure that work is delegated and decisions made closer to the action.
- Place more focus on professional development, linking competency to performance on the job and to continuous improvement.

- Concentrate on learning rather than training. While there is a degree of learning involved in training, training focuses on what to do and how to do it, whereas learning is more concerned with understanding, appreciating, initiating and thinking for yourself. You can link learning to people's performance within the organisation, to stimulate their career development and to assist the organisation to develop.

The power of one

Here are four examples of people who refused to conform, and who created new ways of doing things that changed the nature of the particular activities they were involved in forever.

Jean-Claude Killy

Jean-Claude Killy began skiing at the age of three and by the age of 18 he was a senior member of the French national team. Known as a daring athlete with superb reflexes, he reached speeds of about 130 kilometres an hour. He was the dominant male in this sport from 1966 to 1968. He was the World Cup winner in both 1966–67 and 1967–68 and also led the French team to world championships in those years.

Killy experimented with different ways of moving across a slope to find a competitive edge. He broke the rules by introducing a new skiing style called *avalement* (downhill). This involved two things: skiing with your legs apart instead of together and leaning back instead of forward on sharp turns. The extra speed he gained by using his new method won him the world cups and the triple Olympic crown (downhill, slalom and giant slalom gold medals) at the 1968 Winter Olympics in Grenoble, only the second person to do so. *Avalement* changed skiing forever. However, as we know, nothing is forever, except perhaps nothing. So we wait for the next rule breaker!

Richard Fosbury

Fosbury, American athlete and civil engineer broke the rules and won in another competitive arena: high jumping. Instead of jumping feet first, the conventional way, Fosbury approached the jumping bar at a 45–60 degree angle after a curved run-up and a much faster take-off than normal, and he jumped over it back first. This meant that his head, not his feet, went over the bar first. Thus was born the Fosbury Flop, a radical technique that secured him an Olympic gold medal on 20 October 1968 in Mexico City. Richard's engineering mind was put to excellent athletic use. The Fosbury Flop is the standard high jump technique used today.

Gary Friedman

Gary Friedman is a lawyer and director of the Centre for Mediation in Law in California. His book, *A Guide to Divorce Mediation*, out-lines his approach. He maintains that in many ways, mediation is more painful than divorce because the couple face each other directly. They experience conflict in a very intense way so that mediation is harder.

As a lawyer, Friedman went against the conventions of the legal system, which holds that lawyers should represent only one client. He started to work with both parties, assisting them to reach an agreement that they both considered to be fair. He was keen to avoid bitter battles and court cases, instead trying to reach mutually agreed-upon decisions. Another advantage was to save clients costly legal bills. Thus was born the practice of mediation in civil cases.

Since the early 1980s, he has trained thousands of lawyers in the skills of mediation. He stated that most lawyers are quite attached to law as the standard to be used in determining how people should decide their disputes and don't believe that such a thing as fairness exists. When mediation is brought up, many lawyers are very cyni-cal about it. Instead of being skilled only in litigation, lawyers could now acquire a new set of mediation competencies and help both parties to create solutions. This has changed the way law is practised and provides an alternative to interested parties.

David Warren

Why should a tape recorder stop when it comes to the end of the tape? Today we take continuous loops and automatic play for granted but not so in 1953. That was the year David Warren, an Australian, invented the 'black box', the first flight recorder aircraft instrument. At the time he was working with a team to uncover the cause of a series of British jet airliner crashes. The idea that a tape recorder could run non-stop if it had a continuous wire recorder just popped out at him. The recorder could then collect cockpit conversations right up to the time of an air crash. All he had to do was to ensure the recorder was in a fireproof box (asbestos) and that it could be found easily after the crash. He decided that the tail of the aircraft was the best spot to take the impact of a crash, the shape of the recorder could be round so it would bounce away from the crash site, and it was painted bright orange to make it easy to find. In hindsight it all seems too simple!

Robert Smith

There are many other examples of people breaking the rules and creating new benefits. Breaking the rules or thinking critically is not a negative activity. Think of it as an opportunity to create a new game from an existing one that brings with it new challenges and benefits to people.

Sometimes the rules break by themselves and, *voila!*, serendipity takes its course. The vantage points jump out and something new is born. The stump-jump plough is an example of this.

Some might say the plough is the most important agricultural tool discovered in the history of humans. The earliest one known, which had a metal tip to cut the earth and a container to drop seeds into the furrow, dates back to the Egyptians about 2000 BC.

It all happened one day towards the end of the nineteenth century somewhere in outback South Australia. Robert Smith was ploughing his field when one of the bolts holding the part of the plough that digs into the soil (the mouldboard) snapped. He kept ploughing, hoping it would hold out till he finished. Strangely enough the plough did hold out but in an extraordinary way. There was no slowing down and no stalling, not even over obstacles like half-buried stumps and mallee roots. This broken bolt led to the

development of the 'vixen' in 1876, the first stump-jump plough—
a prototype had won first prize at the Moonta Agricultural Show in
South Australia the previous year.

The improvement which also included an additional lever and
added weight to push the mouldboard down after each jump greatly
reduced costs of farming. A plough that could jump stumps while
operating meant that you did not have to grub (clear) the land of
stumps and roots before ploughing. Grubbing the land was an
extreme toil, dreaded by farmers for the profound exertion required
and crippling costs incurred. An acre of land costing £1 would cost
up to £7 to grub.

Serendipity, perspicacity and learning through observation led
Robert Smith to create the stump-jump plough that transformed
farming practices worldwide, forever.

Creating is learning

You may be surprised to know that when you're absorbed in a
creative activity you're actually being quite highly organised, returning regularly to tasks and sequences already familiar to you so
you can re-examine them to discover a new angle, a new way to
understand a process in an existing situation. Looking for greater
depth and breadth is the aim of creativity. The looking is actually
a learning process. It means making innovative choices about
options. This requires the combined use of imagination and thinking critically.

At its simplest, thinking is a process of remembering. Thinking
critically is remembering and simultaneously asking challenging
questions about recollections. To reflect critically means to try and
reinterpret past experiences. Critical reflection is a process of learning. Learning at its simplest level means being able to remember
things, acquire knowledge, understand new concepts and appreciate them better. We learn when we focus our effort even if it is
simply that we are not progressing.

Learning is a process of *dividing* and of *joining*. Dividing means
duplicating ideas and patterns. This means we learn when we copy

ideas and actions. Joining means going on to use the things we copy and make them our own. In other words, integrating what we duplicate into our existing ways. This synthesis is what we call growth. Growth is not solely doing more of the same things but doing a greater variety of things. This is creativity. The dynamic patterns we adopt through creativity can become more intricate, so the result is a more energetic integration of our thinking with our actions.

Learning improves our ability to detect and correct actions we have judged to be incorrect. This is significant because being correct is an important basis for enhancing confidence and improving potential in ourselves and in our communities.

Ironically, learning is also a process of making mistakes, of steadily modifying our actions in response to a frequently changing environment. Being correct or learning successfully can be equated with matching appropriate actions to situations so the situations have the desired outcomes. In this sense a person who is learning has the ability to do things differently.

Learning is part of a complete process that incorporates training, education and development in its many forms. Remembering, perceiving, analysing, monitoring, adjusting, evaluating, applying, seeing the big picture and acting justly are all forms of development learning.

Knowledge tends to be viewed as a static concept. It is often equated with information and data, but it is much more than that. Knowledge can refer to facts or to a set of ideas and emotions about a situation. It can also refer to a way of doing things. Knowledge can refer to habits of mind and points of view. It can be things we take for granted and are unaware of for much of the day, or it can be gut feelings and intuitions or insights that come to us in a flash. Knowledge includes our sense of what is right, good and useful. It is our sense of the spiritual and our sense of awe. Knowledge can also be a crazy idea or a creative scenario and the endeavours we put into making it a reality.

Intellectual capital is all of this and much more. It is also the routines we put in place to make life easier, happier, more productive and what we want it to be. It includes the way we establish networks and fulfil our needs for companionship in life and in work. It is how we cooperate and share our aspirations and achievements and failures. It is the effort we put into pursuing our curiosities and our passions, our talent as well as the potential we have. It ranges from simple activities, such as observing and sensing, to increasingly complex activities, such as understanding, evaluating, applying and creating. To define intellectual capital is to define what it means to be human. It is not just something in the brain, it is in our heart and a part of our whole being and experience.

Every person is different. So there are trillions of combinations that create intellectual capital. Intellectual capital, also referred to as human capital, is all the knowledge, experience and people performance capacity an organisation may use to create both spiritual and material wealth. For this reason it would seem impossible to measure the replacement costs of a person's intellectual capital. We can measure the cost of training but we cannot measure the amount of learning. Cost is on the input side, the resources we put into an effort. The value created by knowledge is on the output side, the customer side, the value-added side, the side that involves research, thinking, creating and designing. The accounting system designed to measure tangibles cannot give us what we want. We need to change our mindset about measuring and valuing intellectual capital.

Commonsense answers

Commonsense is the capacity to do things most people might do in the same situation. It means relaxing, letting go and going with the flow and not trying to understand it. Commonsense requires a sort of detached attitude. When we let go of personal attachment we are well placed to have open discourse with others who have an interest and some exposure to the issue. Enlightened self-interest, where we can act knowing this is how an enlightened community might act from their reflected experience, is the basis of commonsense. Commonsense arises from a group sense on what is right and is a form of wisdom. It gives us the energy to avoid repetition of foolishness and to focus on alternatives, on likely solutions. Try to:

- challenge the present way of doing things when you know it's not probable or likely to work
- invert the problems you see (turn them backwards, upside down, inside out—play with it in silly ways to see what works
- avoid focusing solely on the end product—enjoy breaking the rules, experiment
- change your state of mind so you feel you are continually learning by regarding issues as challenges and enjoyable adventures
- be excited about everything you do and try to do it with passion
- change one small thing and observe the seemingly invisible—focus carefully on routine and detail that you tend to take for granted
- change the rules of the game—one rule first might be all it needs
- use your intuition
- create new ways
- avoid reacting where you can.

Five suggestions to improve your intellectual capital

1. Observe in different ways

Simply observing seems easy enough, but how difficult can it be to just look and listen? We need to be aware of our thinking and feelings. Is there something we want to see even if it's not there? For example, we want to see a job progressing, so that's what we see, even though the evidence suggests the job is not progressing. When we listen, do we hear only the things we want to hear? We should look for details in a way that might be surprising. Our power of observation limits what we can discover and create. Focusing on these four things will help to sharpen your observation abilities:

- be aware of *how* you observe—for example, do you always look at the same things?
- put yourself totally within the context of who and what you are observing; imagine you're standing in someone else's shoes and try to empathise with their point of view

- express uncertainty and ask people to confirm or, if necessary, correct your impression
- observe with a colleague and share the outcomes—where do you differ and why? There should be some differences!

2. Do things differently

When we do things we should notice more the way we are presently doing them and try a different way. We especially tend not to notice how we do things we are good at. Select something you are naturally good at and try to describe in detail how you do it to someone else. Then change something about it and see what happens. You will find that your awareness of different aspects that are automatic suddenly become noticeable. Next time you go home, unlock the door using the other hand. Open the mail in a way that conserves and allows recycling of plastic versus paper.

3. Take risks

We know if we are taking a risk because we don't feel easy about when we do—we tend to be more careful than usual and check the process to avoid mistakes. Confirm the information that you need is correct to verify the risk. Check the obvious assumptions to ensure you have accurately assessed the risk. Ask yourself what you can do to protect yourself against possible threat from the risk. Identify the first and most important priority in the risk. Consider the implications and consequences. Is there a safer and more productive perspective on the situation rather than seeing it as threatening? Take risks but ensure you know how to protect your-self and others if it is a real risk. That is, take calculated risks!

4. Be true to your values

Some people will speed when driving yet tell everyone they care about safety on the road. Some managers insist they value team-work, cooperation and problem-solving in groups yet they rarely delegate or discuss business issues with other staff or even become a member of any of the work groups—they may even veto consensus decisions they don't like. Ensure what you say you believe in is what you do. Expect others to follow your lead through their observations of what you appear to them.

5. Think critically

We tend not to question the things we believe are correct. It is only when something goes wrong that we do question them. Identify the assumptions that support your actions. Are you surprised by any of your assumptions? As professionals dealing with other people we have an obligation to think critically about things we take for granted and about things that seem to be going well. There is always a better way. Improvement is a never-ending process and continuous improvement will happen if we identify our own assumptions and question them.

Creative destruction

> Clever people master life; the wise illuminate it and create
> fresh difficulties.
> —Emil Nolde, painter and print maker

Successful people are those who are always rebuilding things that work so they will work better! So you should abandon the view that you shouldn't try to fix it if it isn't broken. If you don't dissolve it yourself someone else will and they will also rebuild it. Ask yourself, is it easier to destroy something or to change it? Which is better? Remember, forgetting is a type of destruction. When you abandon and walk away from something it is a passive or mental destruction. You might put it on ice and unfreeze it in the future if you ever need bits of it again. A creative way to destroy something then is to simply forget it, freeze it—like frozen assets.

Our culture tends to focus on the dichotomy of death and life. To avoid this, let's create four perspectives instead of two, taking a leaf from the Hindu pantheon. The Hindu religion has three main gods, a vivid example of the importance placed on destruction, creation and preservation within that culture. There is a time to be born and a time to die as well as a time to preserve. Brahma is the creator; Vishnu the preserver and Shiva the destroyer. For our purposes, we'll add an element that neutralises, a freezer.

We can use these four activators—creator, destroyer, preserver, freezer—as an important framework for thinking critically. The framework avoids the typical dichotomy of good and bad and establishes four vantage points.

Think about your goals in terms of comparisons between what you have and what you want.

- If you want something and don't have it, you will be a creator
- If you have something and don't want it, you will be a destroyer
- If you want something and have it, you will be a preserver
- If you don't have something and don't want it, you will be a freezer.

You can create a grid to list the things you need to create in your work, those you want to destroy, elements you wish to preserve and those that you think have passed their use-by date and need to be frozen. Identifying these factors will be a strong basis for asking basic questions and for challenging some of the assumptions you have. See the chart on the next page, completed by a manager as an example. The chart provides an overview, windows with lists of items identified by the manager, a whole picture of what the manager regards as important to the work being done.

Do a grid for yourself. The more you fit into a window, the greater clarity you will develop about your work. You will come to appreciate exactly how you want to progress. Each window can grow or diminish in size depending on how much focus you wish to place on that role. The freezer role is important because the idea is to put things you do not want and you do not have on ice. Rather than destroy them, it makes those things inert but available through thawing out if you think that there may be some desire for them in the future. If you are making this list as an employer or employee, there is another point of balance that needs to be considered and that is other people. Think of the group but the challenge is to factor in the needs of the individual.

Four windows for thinking critically

YES ↑	**CREATOR** Leadership of a project Autonomy to do the job To be employer of choice Deliver excellence 20 per cent profit increase	**PRESERVER** Use own style with customers Decide on portfolio of clients Image of 'socially responsible' Clean, modern look Dynamic management team
DO YOU WANT IT?	**FREEZER** Management of non-core work Low spend customers Staff with bilingual ability Financial mortgages	**DESTROYER** Unsafe workplace Executives who lack respect HR interference Problem customers
NO ↓		

NO ◄──────── DO YOU HAVE IT? ────────► YES

Turning the
Seven Keys

What is going to change human behaviour is changes in
human thinking. Not changes in human values.
—Edward de Bono, psychologist and author

Every person has their own style of thinking critically which tends
not to change very much over their lifetime unless, of course, they
make a deliberate and sustained effort to refine their style. It is
important not to accept that there is only one way of thinking and
one way to make things happen. Things are not what they seem.
Our capacity for independence in thinking and expression is the
basis of freedom within our democracy.

The Seven Keys to thinking critically represent just a few ways
of approaching the goal of self-improvement in thinking and
expression. Each key is a different type of critical thinking that
works towards opening your mind. The metaphor of a 'key' could
imply a simple action of matching the correct skill with the correct
person and simply turning it to open the door to thinking critically.
This is misleading. Each Key needs to be used many times every
time you want to enter the world of thinking critically in one way.

The Seven Keys are not steps. Nor are they a sequence or hierarchy of actions that encroach on your mental activity. Rather, each
Key is a way of thinking differently. Each Key is a new perspective
on what would otherwise continue to be a routine set of challenges

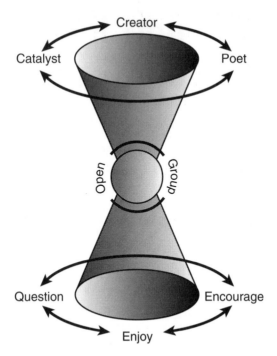

in your daily life. The purpose of the Seven Keys is to help you realise the potential of your thinking style and to develop flexibility and creativity.

The Seven Keys represent important ideas and actions that I have found to be effective in developing critical and creative thinking in children, students, employees and managers at all levels within enterprises. You will need to decide which of these Seven Keys you will incorporate into your thinking style. Initially, select the Keys that seem most user-friendly to you and start to use them, gradually fashioning them into your own style so you emerge as a sharper and more creative person through the various challenges of your life.

Hints to implementing the Keys

The real challenge lies in disciplining yourself to implement the Seven Keys despite the daily pressures of your routine activities.

Should you upset your daily routines by trying to do them differently based on the Seven Keys, or should you practise the Seven Keys in isolation, integrating them slowly after you have a sense of how they work? Here are four hints to help you integrate the Seven Keys into your life habits.

First, aim for a simple start. Find small bite-sized activities that are routine and easy for you to do and think about how to begin your use of the Keys. Second, aim for frequency of interaction with the particular Key you are implementing. Learning a new thinking habit is like learning to play a musical instrument, you need frequent bursts of practice. The practice needs to be careful and at a slow pace initially, ensuring that when you do speed up your thinking you do not become sloppy. It is not much use practising a new thinking skill once or twice a year. What is required is daily practice of the same Key with the same issue or routine activity until you have mastered it. Master the detail. Make your frequent implementation vivid and practical. Vary the pace. Seek feedback from colleagues or friends.

Third, focus on the future and what is possible. It is useful to think of past experiences and learn from them but the Seven Keys are practically oriented, intended to be used with current activites. Try and avoid thinking too much about past experiences. What matters with the Seven Keys is that you engage in real actions that will affect the future and what is possible. Take the long view. Engage in 'pre-flection' (thinking before you act) and plan what you want to learn and achieve from particular activities that are the hub of your thoughts.

Fourth, track your own learning and progress. I encourage you to assess your critical reflection skills using CRI exercise by asking a friend or colleague to assess your skills. You could repeat this assessment every six months. In addition, monitor how you approach particular tasks and if you lost opportunities to use any of the Keys you are practising. It is well known from research into adult learning that people learn more if they direct and monitor their own progress. So, become a self-directed learner and then help others to achieve this important independence.

What is important to remember is that you are a catalyst for yourself. You need to speed up the reaction between your thoughts and activities in a way that incorporates thinking differently into your own thinking style. While you master this for yourself you can also be a catalyst for others and for all the groups of which you are a member. To teach is to learn twice. When you try to explain different ways of thinking critically you'll come to understand it better for yourself.

You will find that in work and social groups there are always lots of assumptions to challenge. Traditional wisdom, thinking and acting in predictable routine ways, are deeply entrenched within our work places and leisure venues. You will always find some policy, people or procedures that prevent you from exploring and thinking laterally. The obstacles to thinking critically are surmountable. People are ready to tell you what you cannot do before they tell you what is possible. At this level it will be the Key of thinking critically in groups that will achieve the best results. Sometimes the best way to dislodge the wall of unhelpful wisdom is to garner the forces of the group and to put in place new systems. This requires that the group re-frames the situation. Behaviour and thinking and the expression of these occur through the language we use.

We need to maximise the use of the Seven Keys by revisiting the way we express our thinking through our language and through our behaviours. Language, thinking and behaviour are all enmeshed and we need to approach creativity and thinking critically from all of these perspectives. We need to share our recurring thought patterns through different language and different behaviours. You will need to decide which of the Seven Keys to use to help you achieve this. Swap and change them as you go, try them all.

> Responding to change means we have to change—constantly.
> —Sue Vardon, CEO, Centrelink

Remember, the Seven Keys are vantage points; they help you clarify perspective through contrast. The psychologist Jerome Bruner said, 'The fish is the last to discover water'. Only when you take the fish out of the water to experience the shock of the atmosphere can it appreciate the life giving force of its own environment. The Seven Keys encourage you to march out of step, to hop, to skip and to run, to stand still and to jump. Delight in life through thinking critically.

We need a fresh mindset and to believe there is new territory for us to discover. We have to make a new map and that requires new ways of behaving. We can't walk on snow the same way we walk on the tar road. The snow under our feet draws them down in a way we cannot prevent, so we walk differently as a reaction. Can we walk like this in our own territory? Can we tiptoe along the same ground that we walk, stride, roll, shuffle along or perhaps walk on our hands?'

Profile of a critical thinker

I would like to finish this section with some personal information given to me by Robert Black, a person I've only met on the infosphere. He asked me to participate in helping him develop his creativity test. I did. Robert's creativity test is experimental and anyone can access it by visiting his website at *www.cre8ng.com*. The test gives a profile of your reported preferences for creativity and reactions to simple questions. It is unlike the CRI. Robert, a creativity guru, supplied me with this sample description based on answers that I selected to his multiple-choice questions. It's a fair profile for a person who is intent on critical thinking:

> Your basic approach to thinking involves variability and uniqueness. When you are learning something new you prefer to work alone and explore the new material, but in selected cases you prefer the group. When trying to solve problems you generally choose to work on many projects and create numbers of solutions. When you communicate you generally use pictures and are energetic.
>
> Experimentation, new methods or ways to do things or to create new ideas greatly interest you. A project here, a project there, a project somewhere else—this describes how you prefer

to work. Conceptualising, seeking new possibilities even for unknown problems are your greatest strengths. Hunches, imaginary flights, flashes are as valid as facts and figures to you. Four words distinctly describe you: intuitive, imaginative, innovative and insightful. Your finest solutions have often come from insights. You walk to a different drum when it comes to taking chances about what you 'know' or 'feel' will work. Explorations, flights of fantasy, unknown trips prove to help you learn.

You tend to be a person who likes to try a variety of things or you like to do old things in new ways. Your friends or relatives would probably label you as creative. You are probably a strong risk taker and roll very well with the punches life gives you. You have a strong tendency to be a loner or selective about the people who you spend time with. You can work alone very easily. You prefer work that is challenging and out of the ordinary. Having to do the same type of work day-in, day-out would be boring and/or stressful for you.

You are probably a private kind of person, who keeps their emotions to themselves. However, you don't mind being around friendly people, even if they get personable and clown around. Teamwork, when everyone agrees on specific tasks to accomplish, is not difficult or uncomfortable for you. The indication is that you enjoy to work with things, ideas, and systems as well as with people.

The following words tend to describe probable strengths of yours: intuitive, synthesiser, original, flexible, loner/joiner, empathic, multiple possibilities.

The following words tend to describe possible weaknesses of yours: exaggerate, take too many risks for others, get lost in concepts and dreams, seen as not fitting in, very enthusiastic.

If you have perused this far it means you will probably continue. Part Two is entirely different from what you have experienced so far! But I hope you will find intellectual and emotional delights that will convince you even further to *open your mind* to the oceanic depths of our human capabilities. It wasn't until I visited my place of birth, Gioia Tauro, a small seaside town in Reggio Calabria on the tip of Italy's toe, that I experienced a deep blue Mediterranean ocean! Now, that is a cerulean ocean! Part Two of this book is designed to 'enchant' your imagination with new and profound tones. Appreciate the deep sea! Appreciate the richness of thinking critically.

PART TWO

THINKING ABOUT THINKING

1 I think, therefore I am

Imagination is the beginning of creation. You imagine what you desire; you will what you imagine; and at last you create what you will.
—George Bernard Shaw, dramatist

Thinking gives us our identity. Our collective thinking creates what is good and what is unacceptable in our particular culture. We form a view of ourselves through talking to other people and living and working together with them. We usually prefer to surround ourselves with like-minded people, people who will reflect back to us the kind of person we want to be. In many ways we are the product of our environment and how we are genetically programmed to respond to our world.

Thinking is the particular way you manage your thoughts, feelings and intuitions.
—Francesco Sofo

Some people believe in destiny. Others believe they can control what they do and what happens to them. Deeply held beliefs and values are difficult if not nearly impossible to change. First, you need to acknowledge the belief you hold with clarity—that is, identify it clearly. Then you need to acknowledge the good reasons you have for maintaining the belief. Of course, the difficulty here is that beliefs tend to defy rationality—we all maintain beliefs in spite of valid reasons to abandon them. People will maintain a belief simply because it feels right so intuition is a strong substitute for our weakest reason. History and habit are also formidable forces that entrench our beliefs. The truth is that thinking critically has impregnable enemies and a simple yet strongly held belief is one of those enemies. The Seven Keys to critical thinking are designed to help you manage your thoughts, feelings and intuitions effectively in spite of the obstacles.

Thinking is valued in our society. If you have a high Intelligence Quotient (IQ) it means you are smart and that you may be given a scholarship, lots of attention and opportunities. You may win mathematics Olympiads, chess tournaments or quiz shows or come top of your class. High scores will open many doors and allow you to take up the best job of your choice. But the IQ test is only one way of measuring intelligence; however, education systems have an unfortunate habit of changing very slowly and have difficulty keeping up with the advances in technology, communication and the social arena. For this reason the IQ test, which is culturally bound to a specific society, becomes outdated and restrictive, especially if used within an education system characterised by diversity. Many people who are intelligent don't know what their IQ is. And many who have been told they have a high IQ don't realise their full potential because they don't use their intelligence to best advantage.

Albert Einstein, physicist and Nobel Prize winner, was a great and original thinker; however, he was not very good at school and failed his exams more than once. The reason was that he would not think in the way his teachers wanted him to think. For example, when asked, 'How many feet are there in a mile?' he replied, 'I don't know. Why should I fill my brain with facts that I can find in two minutes in any standard reference book?' In other words, he thought our minds should be used for thinking rather than for just regurgitating facts.

Through our thinking we create our reality

> Watch your thoughts as they become your words. Watch your words as they become your actions. Watch your actions as they become your habits. Watch your habits as they become your character. Watch your character; it becomes your destiny.
> —Frank Outlaw, author

Managing your thoughts involves the particular ways you organise, control and communicate your feelings, intuitions and beliefs. When you organise your thoughts you use special patterns or filters that allow you to understand the world in your own distinctive way. Habits are a good example of the way we do this. Often we respond automatically to a situation without really thinking about it. You have probably been told, 'Think before you speak', or, 'Don't put your foot in your mouth'. Or perhaps you have thought about someone else, 'They're not saying what they mean'. These expressions remind us that we can separate mental activity from what we say and do. We can think one thing but say or do another. Of course this can be a great advantage to human beings! Leo Rosten, an American Polish-born scholar and author of *The Joys of Yiddish*, once said that, 'tact is thinking all you say without saying all you think'.

In many cases we may agree with the ways the world is controlled and are happy to live within that framework. If you haven't been a critical thinker up to now, you may give more importance to what others say than to your own instincts. Critical thinking does make an important difference. We can either accept what others say and what they try to get us to do or we can find our own voice. Thoughts *can* change the world when we act on them energetically.

Some different ways to think about thinking

What is thinking? It's as basic as being aware. Listening, speaking and reading involve thinking. When we listen we focus our mind and pay attention to what others are saying to us. You cannot truly listen without thinking about what you hear. When we speak we express thoughts. We can say one thought while thinking of something different. Some people can think lots of thoughts almost simultaneously as thoughts can occur to us very rapidly or very slowly. Reading is thinking because we are interpreting symbols and diagrams. So thinking means making sense of the world, not just remembering things.

American industrialist and car designer Henry Ford was accused of being a dunce by the *Chicago Tribune* when he was not able to answer the quiz-type questions the newspaper had challenged him with. His response was that while he didn't know the answers to the questions, in five minutes he would be able to find a person who did have those answers. Like Einstein (see above), Henry Ford could not remember lots of facts very well but he knew how to find information quickly when he needed it. Both Einstein and Ford illustrate for us a view that thinking means the ability to solve problems such as accessing information. In other words, thinking is researching, inquiring or simply just finding out.

Einstein and Ford were just two people whose ideas changed the way we live. It has been said that we live on the shoulders of giants and it is true that many useful ideas are passed down from generation to generation. Original thinkers in our time try to build a better and better civilisation. Of course, we should also be mindful that more than 90 per cent of all good ideas go undeveloped to the graves with their creators.

Hunches and intuition are an important part of thinking. Famous inventors may have vast stores of knowledge to call upon but they also have the ability to dream, to visualise and to imagine. This ability is the first step to creating ideas. The next step is to bring the idea to life for others and for ourselves. Ideas do not necessarily live forever. They die and other new ideas are born. The birth process happens after there has been the conception of the idea and then its development to a differentiated and viable idea.

Using all our senses

When we start to think critically and creatively, rather than following well-worn habits, we become aware of our whole body, our whole effort. In fact, all our senses are involved in thinking: sight, hearing, smell, taste and touch. We can also think beyond our senses. Part of thinking is effort, enthusiasm and interest. Thinking requires mental focus and this requires perseverance—we need to keep applying ourselves until we get a result.

Levels of personal energy are an important part of our thinking and of who we are. Energy is a relative force and individuals and groups need to decide for themselves when their effort is at a maximum or when it is stressful. Maintaining a focus on a topic, theme or task is a skill anyone can learn even if they have low levels of energy. Harry Emerson Fosdick, an American Baptist minister, said that, 'No steam or gas ever drives anything until it is confined. No Niagara is ever turned into light and power until it is tunnelled. No life ever grows great until it is focused, dedicated, disciplined'. Author R.D. Clyde reminds us that sometimes not focusing too much can give you the result you want: 'It's amazing how long it takes to complete something you're not working on'. He also said that getting things done is not always what is most important. There is value in allowing others to learn, even if the tasks are not accomplished as quickly, efficiently or effectively.

Where low levels of energy are difficult to sustain and to focus you would need to get to the cause of low energy: is it a bad diet, stress, overworking, tiredness? Carl Lewis, the Olympic runner, reminds us that nothing will dissolve the deficiencies of a person except hard work, concentration and continued application: 'My thoughts before a big race are usually pretty simple. I tell myself, get out of the block, run your race, stay relaxed. If you run your race, you'll win. Channel your energy. Focus.' The interesting point is where he says 'stay relaxed', which does not concentrate the command to 'focus'. Here is another example of how matching your energy level to the situation is important, and at the end of the day any level of energy can be creative!

Thomas Edison, the inventor, was able to turn a scar into a star. He always had the feeling that his poor capacity to focus on a single task was the origin of his creative efforts. Like Einstein, Edison had great difficulties in school and dropped out, going from one job to another until he created his own career of inventor, which matched his own levels of energy and his own particular thinking style. At one stage in his life he was working on over 40 different inventions at the same time, keeping his own schedule of working hours that made him very productive.

Reflections

Thinking is a unique activity. It acts like a mirror to itself. *We can actually think about our thinking.* When we guide our thinking we are using it to full advantage and at the same time maintaining it. Thinking has the capacity for self-maintenance and upgrades itself to work in new ways. This is because thinking can look back into itself and regenerate itself. How amazing is that!

When we are able to think and dream in different ways from the ways we are used to then we will have acquired something of great value, something that will help us to achieve what our hearts and our minds desire.

To truly live the life we want to live means choosing, and this involves making judgements. As Jean-Paul Sartre, the French philosopher and novelist, said, 'You are your choices'.

2 What's your critical thinking profile?

I used to think the human brain was the most fascinating part
of the body, and then I realized, 'What is telling me that?'
—Emo Phillips, comedian

Take a deep breath. You're about to take your first step on the journey to becoming a critical thinker. Or it might be the next step on
your continuing quest to becoming a more effective critical thinker.
Whether you're a novice or a practised thinker, you'll need to know
how you rate in your own perception, and the perception of other
people. Other people's perceptions of us are vital in coming to
know ourselves better. The ones who have the most impact on our
identity, self-image and self-esteem are our most significant others,
which usually include close family, friends and colleagues that we
respect.

The definition of thinking critically given earlier is the *capacity
to identify and challenge assumptions*. There are at least six skills
required to be able to develop this capacity to a comfortable level.
The Critical Reflection Inventory (CRI) is a self-rating question-
naire that uses these six dimensions, which are summarised in the
acronym CODE ON:

Cognitive awareness
Observation
Difference
Empathy
Openness
Non-personalisation.

Increasing your *cognitive* (mental) *awareness* is the first step to improving your skills. It makes you attentive of the importance of different points of view, your habit of mind and how you might change your behaviour. Better mental awareness is a skill that increases your capacity to appreciate yourself, others and the many environments that impact on you—social, emotional, physical, political, economic, geographical, technological, communicational and cultural.

How much do you really notice and what is the quality of your *observations*? Observing length, height and width—that is, quantity, quality and beyond—and taking the long view is the second dimension of thinking critically. Valuing *difference* is the third important aspect. This means striving for variation in routine actions and happily seeking out different ideas and practices. The fourth dimension of *empathy* refers to the interface points in your interactions with others and includes both thinking and feeling in synergy with others.

Openness, the fifth skill is pivotal to thinking critically. All other skills emanate from openness. This is the capacity for integrity about one's own assumptions and a willingness to respect other points of view. It also means acceptance that more than one solution exists. The sixth skill measured on the CRI is *non-personalisation*, the ability to deal with issues separately and together while accounting for the emotional factors. Thinking critically has its role in being dispassionate.

The prime purpose of the CRI is to help you become more aware of how you think about your own skills in thinking critically. It is desirable to have skills in all six areas of thinking critically measured in the CRI. Work through the following exercise to find out your CRI score.

Your critical reflection inventory (CRI)

The following is a list of 24 statements about critical reflection. Read each statement and circle the number that most accurately matches your present behaviour. A rating of 1 indicates you *never* engage in that behaviour while a rating of 6 indicates you *always* behave in the manner described.

1	2	3	4	5	6
Never	Hardly ever	Some-times	Often	Nearly always	Always

Circle one number for each statement

1. When solving problems, I do not mind if the other person has priorities that are different from mine.   1 2 3 4 5 6

2. I do not become anxious if someone opposes my views.   1 2 3 4 5 6

3. I am sensitive to others' feelings.   1 2 3 4 5 6

4. I am accurate in my observations.   1 2 3 4 5 6

5. I do not make decisions on impulse.   1 2 3 4 5 6

6. I am open minded.   1 2 3 4 5 6

7. When solving problems I evaluate the pros and cons of different options.   1 2 3 4 5 6

8. I do not feel attacked when presented with opinions different from my own.   1 2 3 4 5 6

9. I can sense when others react strongly.   1 2 3 4 5 6

10. I examine the way I think so I can make my thinking more accurate.   1 2 3 4 5 6

11. I think carefully about problems rather than act on impulse.   1 2 3 4 5 6

12. I know how I am feeling when I am dealing with issues.   1 2 3 4 5 6

13. I am sensitive to others' ideas.   1 2 3 4 5 6

14. I am afraid to bring conflicting points of view out into the open.   1 2 3 4 5 6

15. I am good at making sense of other people's behaviour.   1 2 3 4 5 6

16. I can interpret the same situation in different ways.   1 2 3 4 5 6

17. I know when other people are confused.   1 2 3 4 5 6

18. I change my beliefs if I find they are not worthwhile.   1 2 3 4 5 6

19. I can engage with how others see things.   1 2 3 4 5 6

20. I don't become defensive when others reject my ideas.   1 2 3 4 5 6

21. When making observations I am aware of my biases.   1 2 3 4 5 6

22. I can describe many aspects of what I observe.   1 2 3 4 5 6

23. I have noticed a shift in myself towards being more open minded.   1 2 3 4 5 6

24. I question my own assumptions.   1 2 3 4 5 6

How to score

1. Each column represents one of the six dimensions of critical reflection. Record the rating from each of the 24 statements above in the correct CODE ON column below. For example, your rating for question 1 should be added to the D column.

2. Add the ratings of the four statements in each CODE ON column. The total of the four ratings in each column should be between 4 and 24.

Cognitive awareness	Observation	Difference	Empathy	Openness	Non-personalisation
C	**O**	**D**	**E**	**O**	**N**
Q5 =	Q4 =	Q1 =	Q3 =	Q6 =	Q2 =
Q11 =	Q10 =	Q7 =	Q9 =	Q12 =	Q8 =
Q17 =	Q16 =	Q13 =	Q15 =	Q18 =	Q14 =
Q23 =	Q22 =	Q19 =	Q21 =	Q24 =	Q20 =
Total =	Total =	Total =	Total =	Total =	Total =

3. Transfer the total for each of the six columns from the table above to each CODE ON letter listed below. The minimum total of all six dimensions of the CRI should be no less than 24 while the maximum should be no more than 144.

(C) ____ +   (O) ____ +   (D) ____ +   (E) ____ +

(O) ____ +   (N) ____ =   (Sum total) _____

4. Fill in you total score on the CRI Score Summary Sheet on the next page, then mark your self-rating score on each dimension with a cross X.

How to interpret your score

The dimension with the lowest total is the one you perceive as being your least used skill in the area of critical thinking. The dimension with the highest total is the one you regard as being your most used critical thinking skill. A difference of more than eight points between the highest and lowest on any of the six dimensions indicates a lack of flexibility in using your least regarded critical thinking ability. Totals within four points of each other indicate flexibility in using those dimensions of critical reflection.

Cognitive awareness

A high score indicates you believe you understand and acknowledge your own thinking strengths and limitations while you actually engage in thinking about problems. You have probably noticed you tend to lean towards being open rather than closed to ideas different from your own. You are likely to think very carefully about issues and possible solutions rather than to make decisions on impulse. This means that you will probably notice other peoples' thought processes as well as your own and are able to recognise confusion or muddled thinking in relation to problems. You are conscious of your specific levels of competence and incompetence in the way you think while you are thinking.

CRI SCORE SUMMARY SHEET

Name: _____ Date: _____

Your CRI total score is: _____

COGNITIVE AWARENESS
To what extent do you understand your own thinking?

Low   High

4 5 6 7 8 9 10 11 12 13 14 15 16 17 18 19 20 21 22 23 24

OBSERVATION
To what extent do you make accurate observations from many angles?

4 5 6 7 8 9 10 11 12 13 14 15 16 17 18 19 20 21 22 23 24

DIFFERENCE
To what extent do you value differences?

4 5 6 7 8 9 10 11 12 13 14 15 16 17 18 19 20 21 22 23 24

EMPATHY
To what extent can you appreciate others' feelings and behaviours?

4 5 6 7 8 9 10 11 12 13 14 15 16 17 18 19 20 21 22 23 24

OPENNESS
To what extent do you identify and challenge assumptions?

4 5 6 7 8 9 10 11 12 13 14 15 16 17 18 19 20 21 22 23 24

NON-PERSONALISATION
To what extent do you not become defensive or attack others?

4 5 6 7 8 9 10 11 12 13 14 15 16 17 18 19 20 21 22 23 24

Observation

If you scored well in this dimension you regard yourself as being able to perceive and interpret events from many points of view. You notice detail and you are comfortable making accurate observations of the same phenomenon from different perspectives while simultaneously endeavouring to critically refine your own thinking processes by noticing your own ways of perceiving and thinking.

Difference

A high total in this dimension means you recognise the importance of difference in your routine behaviour. As well, when approaching problem solving you actively seek different opinions and encourage others who have different values from your own. You are comfortable in engaging with different perspectives and remain responsive to different ideas.

Empathy

If you have a high score in this dimension then you see yourself as naturally demonstrating your appreciation of other peoples' frames of reference, habits of mind and points of view. You value what others think, communicate and feel and you show them that this is indeed the case. You can easily detect and interpret accurately others' feelings and behaviours because you are genuinely aware of your own frame of reference. You are able to appreciate diversity and uniqueness in thinking.

Openness

If you rate highly here, you feel you are skilled in subjective reframing—that is, you have the ability to identify and challenge your own assumptions. In fact, questioning your own assumptions would come easily to you. You remain open to change and improvement in the area of your own ideas and feelings and would consider changing them if you find they are not useful or worthwhile. When you are confronted with good reasons contrary to your own point of view you do not remain closed to them. You endeavour to develop a level of mutual respect whereby ideas become shared. Becoming open to ways of thinking other than your own demonstrates that such sharing has occurred out of a context of mutual respect.

You have come to respect the point of view of others. You have thus arrived at the most advanced stage of critical reflection.

Non-personalisation

Scoring well in this dimension indicates you are easily able to deal with issues while separating them from their personal aspects. Your normal reaction is not to become anxious when someone else opposes your claims and not to feel personally attacked. You have an attitude of welcoming the opportunity to debate the pros and cons of each other's opinion. You tend to try to embrace conflicting points of view and to consider others' reasons for opposing and rejecting your ideas. That is, you are able to distinguish between 'enemies' and problems. In fact, your attitude is not to consider people who disagree with you as antagonists, instead you perceive them as challenges because problems tend to persist after 'enemies' are vanquished. Oppressive cultural practices are much bigger than single individuals or groups and most problems tend to be systemic rather than emanating from single opponents. You focus on the issues at hand rather than divert your energy into going into battle with your critics. You are a pragmatist, realising that adopting a confrontative attitude towards rivals among your colleagues would only prevent or delay solutions.

> We are the hurdles we leap to be ourselves.
> —Michael McClure, poet, novelist, essayist, playwright

The ideal result of the inventory is a balance of all six dimensions— that is, a similar score. From here, select which critical reflection dimensions you feel you need to develop further and look back through the statements to identify specific skills you can practise more often so you can be more comfortable and have greater flexibility in using all dimensions of thinking critically.

After considering your profile individually, decide how accurate you think it is. Then ask a close colleague, such as your work supervisor, a good friend or partner, to complete the CRI Observer Rating Scale below for you.

OBSERVER CRITICAL REFLECTION INVENTORY (CRI)

Name: _____ **Date:** _____

The following is a list of 24 statements about critical reflection. Read each statement and circle the number that most accurately matches the behaviour of the person whose name appears above. A rating of 1 indicates you think the person *never* engages in that behaviour while a rating of 6 indicates you think he or she *always* behaves in the manner described.

Circle one number for each statement

1	2	3	4	5	6
Never	Hardly ever	Some-times	Often	Nearly always	Always

1. When solving problems, s/he does not mind if the other person has priorities that are different from hers/his.   1 2 3 4 5 6
2. S/he does not become anxious if someone opposes her/his views.   1 2 3 4 5 6
3. S/he is sensitive to others' feelings.   1 2 3 4 5 6
4. S/he is accurate in their observations.   1 2 3 4 5 6
5. S/he does not make decisions on impulse.   1 2 3 4 5 6
6. S/he is open minded.   1 2 3 4 5 6
7. When solving problems s/he evaluates the pros and cons of different options.   1 2 3 4 5 6

8. S/he does not feel attacked when presented with opinions different from their own.   1 2 3 4 5 6

9. S/he can sense when others react strongly.   1 2 3 4 5 6

10. S/he examines the way s/he thinks so s/he can make their thinking more accurate.   1 2 3 4 5 6

11. S/he thinks carefully about problems rather than act on impulse.   1 2 3 4 5 6

12. S/he knows how s/he is feeling when dealing with issues.   1 2 3 4 5 6

13. S/he is sensitive to others' ideas.   1 2 3 4 5 6

14. S/he is afraid to bring conflicting points of view out into the open.   1 2 3 4 5 6

15. S/he is good at making sense of other people's behaviour.   1 2 3 4 5 6

16. S/he can interpret the same situation in different ways.   1 2 3 4 5 6

17. S/he knows when other people are confused.   1 2 3 4 5 6

18. S/he can change her/his beliefs if s/he finds they are not worthwhile.   1 2 3 4 5 6

19. S/he can engage with how others see things.   1 2 3 4 5 6

20. S/he doesn't become defensive when others reject her/his ideas.   1 2 3 4 5 6

21. When making observations s/he is aware of her/his biases.   1 2 3 4 5 6

22. S/he can describe many aspects of what s/he observes.   1 2 3 4 5 6

23. S/he has noticed a shift in herself/himself towards being more open minded.   1 2 3 4 5 6

24. S/he question his/her own assumptions.   1 2 3 4 5 6

Fill in the rating below from your colleague's answers about you.

Cognitive awareness	Observation	Difference	Empathy	Openness	Non-personalisation
C	O	D	E	O	N
Q5 =	Q4 =	Q1 =	Q3 =	Q6 =	Q2 =
Q11 =	Q10 =	Q7 =	Q9 =	Q12 =	Q8 =
Q17 =	Q16 =	Q13 =	Q15 =	Q18 =	Q14 =
Q23 =	Q22 =	Q19 =	Q21 =	Q24 =	Q20 =
Total =	Total =	Total =	Total =	Total =	Total =

Transfer the total for each of the six columns to the CODE ON letter below.

(C) ____ + (O) ____ + (D) ____ + (E) ____ +
(O) ____ + (N) ____ = (Sum total) _____

Mark the other person's results on your CRI Score Summary Sheet, but instead of using an X, use a 0 (zero) to signify Other, and a different coloured pen so you can easily distinguish your scores from your friend's.

How to interpret the opinions of your observer

> The moment anyone gives close attention to anything, even a blade of grass, it becomes a mysterious, awesome, indescribably magnificent world in itself.
> —Henry Miller, author

What if their score is vastly different from your own score? A detailed discussion will illuminate the situation. Either they are wrong and don't really know your own capacity for critical thinking or they are right and you don't really know yourself. Another alternative is that both of you know you quite well but in different contexts or perhaps you are both wrong as neither of you knows you very well. Perhaps the values you both have are quite different and so each interprets the same action in very different ways.

In discussing your critical thinking profile you can try to focus on four different areas. The first area is the 'unknown', those aspects about yourself that you and the other person are not aware of yet; you can decrease the unknown by sharing experiences and seeking feedback on your behaviour. The second area is the open corner; these are things you and the other person know about: things you are open about to others through self-disclosure and through shared experiences and feedback. These shared experiences have led to developing mutually satisfying relationships. The third aspect to discuss is the blind spots, those aspects about yourself that you are unaware of that are apparent to the other person; listen carefully and be receptive to what the other person says to you. A fourth area to discuss is your concealment areas, the façade section of your behaviour that includes aspects of yourself you are aware of that the other person is definitely unaware of; you can choose to use self-disclosure or to keep things to yourself.

Thinking critically then is quite a personal thing where you can choose how much you will disclose about yourself, how much information you seek from others about your own behaviour or performance, how much you share about your experiences and how separate you will keep yourself from others. Whatever choices you make in relation to these aspects, people will form an opinion of you whether you like it or not. You need to decide how much you want to actively influence that opinion, if it matters to you and how satisfying you want your interpersonal relationships to be.

It is important to know what other people think of your ability to think critically because we all have the tendency to be deceived by our own opinions. Unless we compare ourselves with others how can we truly be sure our opinions and beliefs are our own or if they are accurate? We need to think with freedom and originality about ourselves, but in particular we need to think with accuracy. Additionally, most people find this a humbling experience.

Quick thinking style quiz

Let's summarise your thinking style profile. I will bombard you with questions and I want to make you *really* think critically about yourself. Write your answers down on a separate piece of paper so you can think about them later as well as now. Some questions may appear to be difficult but try to think about the situation—even if you don't have an answer the question may prompt you to think about it the next time you confront this situation.

- To what extent do you see yourself as an independent thinker?
- When was the last time you changed a belief that you held dearly?
- What about the beliefs held by your friends and colleagues—do you recognise when they change deeply held beliefs and opinions?
- Has your opinion of friends and colleagues not changed at all?
- How deeply do you know and understand your close friends and colleagues?
- Do you know what sources of information and experience your friends and colleagues rely upon to help them shape their particular beliefs and opinions?
- Are any of your friends independent thinkers?
- Who is the most independent thinker you know?
- What qualities make that person original?
- Do you learn from your own successes more than you learn from your failures?
- How do you make the most of your experience, whether it is happy or unhappy?
- How well do you really know yourself?
- How aware are you of the way you think?
- Are you constantly aware of the fact that you are thinking every minute of the day or are you too busy thinking to *know* how you are thinking?
- Do your friends think you are aware of how you are thinking while you are having conversations with them—that is, do they comment on your thinking abilities?
- Are you aware of how your friends think while they are conversing with you and do you think they are monitoring their own thinking while conversing?
- Do you think much about the kudos and accolades great thinkers receive and would *you* like to gain similar recognition?

- What drives your wish to be a creative thinker?
- Are you focused on gaining varied and relevant experience to build your foundation for good thinking?
- Can you reflect on experience to learn?
- Are you able to contribute to the good of society and to your own further enlightenment?

Quick self-assessment

Here is a quick self-assessment of your critical thinking skills. Be open and honest with yourself. Rate each of the six items from 1 to 6. Number 1 means you *never* engage in that behaviour while number 6 means you *always* engage in that behaviour.

I know when I am thinking well and when I am thinking poorly.	1 2 3 4 5 6
My closest friends would agree that I know when I am thinking well and when I am thinking poorly.	1 2 3 4 5 6
I have keen observation skills and am open to learning from my observations.	1 2 3 4 5 6
My closest friends would describe me as a keen observer and open to learning from my observations.	1 2 3 4 5 6
I change deeply held beliefs or opinions through experience.	1 2 3 4 5 6
My closest friends would agree that I change deeply held beliefs or opinions through experience.	1 2 3 4 5 6
I welcome ambiguity and complexity and appreciate those who express these views.	1 2 3 4 5 6
My closest friends would agree that I welcome ambiguity and complexity and appreciate those who express these views.	1 2 3 4 5 6

I accurately express other people's points of
views and articulate good reasons to support
those views.   1 2 3 4 5 6

My closest friends would agree that I accurately
express other people's points of views and
articulate good reasons to support those views. 1 2 3 4 5 6

I can solve problems calmly.   1 2 3 4 5 6

My closest friends would agree that I solve
problems without emotional adversity.   1 2 3 4 5 6

Add the scores of each row and multiply the total by 2.

_____ (Total) × 2 = _____ (Max. 144)

Compare this score to your previous CRI total. Also compare it with
that of your friend or colleague's total for you on the CRI. If all three
scores are about the same, you have made an accurate assessment
about your own critical thinking skills.

Summary and analysis

List your areas of strength and your areas for further development.
You can use the questions below to help you determine this.
Identify and note any areas of congruence and incongruence
between your own perceptions and those of other observers.

Areas of strength
• Determine your basic strengths in critical thinking.
• Which of these are you most comfortable with?
• Which of these do you not feel confident about?
• Why?

Areas for further development
• Which areas do you feel you need to improve?
• In which areas do you most lack confidence?
• What can you do to improve your skills in these areas?

Action plan

> 'Now thyself' is more important than 'Know thyself'.
> —Mel Brooks, comedic filmmaker

This is an action step—it is an opportunity for you to focus your mind on the present and to become consciously and fully aware of your own thinking.

If you had a low score on Cognitive Awareness you may feel you need to improve your awareness of your own mental skills. You might try to create space at meal times, before or after, to reflect on problems. What things concern you? How did you think about them? Try and create a picture of the way you see yourself thinking. Do you see your mind working like an old time clock with cogs and springs or do you see yourself as a modern watch with a computer chip where things are 'yes, no', 'yes, no' and only one can win?

If you had a low score on Observation then try and notice unusual things. Do some puzzles in newspapers where you have to spot the differences between two pictures that look exactly the same. Notice what clothes your colleagues wear everyday. Tell them if you notice they have a new colour in their hair. Try and observe the way others begin their conversations with you. Do they say, 'Hi' and then talk, or do they just start to talk without warning? Look to notice things you would not normally think of noticing.

If you have a problem accepting other people's ideas, you could try to listen more, argue less, expose yourself to different points of view more often and become more informed. Here is a way of measuring your progress.

Study the table below and enter the skill you wish to improve, the date you want to try to change your behaviour by, the type of strategies you will use and how you expect to be different in terms of how you will know that you have improved the skills: what will you see, hear and feel about things that are different from the way you see, hear and feel about things now.

Thinking critically skill that I wish to improve	Date of improvement	Strategies I will use to improve skill	Things I will see, hear and feel differently
Cognitive awareness			
Observation			
Difference			
Empathy			
Openness			
Non-personalisation			

This table will help you focus and act on your strengths and weaknesses to improve your ability to think critically.

3 A close look at thinking critically

It is a natural thing in the brain to seek symmetry. I don't feel that compulsion. There is the notion that if you find the ultimate answer everything springs from it. But I don't think it does.
—Edward de Bono, critical thinker

An increased capacity to focus your thoughts and your beliefs will allow you to achieve your goals coherently. This is because you will have identified some of your own biases, will have explored situations from different points of views and will have identified good reasons for adopting any of those directions.

As individuals we all need to apply good reasoning skills with a renewed sense of curiosity, fervent fascination and elegant imagination. Existing habits become challenges for creative approaches when *we can keep reinventing what we do* and *how we do it*.

There are three major aspects to thinking critically, which are connected. Thinking critically embraces **reason**, explores **assumption** and creates a fresh **perspective** that leads to *new ways of doing things*.

- Reason has two aspects—**reasonableness** (fairness) and **reasoning** (logical, valid and correctly deduced).
- Assumptions can be **explicit** (stated) and **implicit** (unstated).
- Perspectives can be **your own** and those of **others**.

Let's look at these skills and discover ways in which you can improve them.

Reasoning

> We still believe that winning an argument, proving you're
> right, proving someone else is wrong, is sufficient. It is not.
> —Edward de Bono, inventor of term 'lateral thinking'

When you discover a problem in the flow of an argument, you are thinking critically. To uncover problems in the course of a conversation you can focus on two things, the reasonableness and the reasoning.

To put forward a sound argument, you'll need to be reasonable while you are reasoning. This may sound odd because we expect reasoning—the process of drawing conclusions from the available evidence—to be reasonable; that is, showing sound judgement. However, we know this is not true in all cases. For example, 'because I like to' may be a good *reason* for choosing to wear your swimming costume but it's not a *reasonable* judgement to wear your swimming costume to the office. In other words, other factors contribute to the judgement of what is a good reason. To be robust, reasons needs to be both rigorous *and* reasonable.

Using reasoning: the umbrella

> I am taking my umbrella with me because the weather
> forecast is for a hot and sunny day.

On the surface this statement does not sound like a reasonable statement. However, if experience has proved differently then the reason might be judged fair and good. For example, the weather bureau forecast hot and sunny conditions for the past three days but there have been unexpected showers every day.

To be reasonable you must agree on what makes the reasons good and fair. To be reasoning or logical you must clarify the reasons. If the reasons are stated, you need to simply clarify your own understanding. If the reasons are not stated because people assume they are obvious or because they are not sure what the reasons are, then you need to ask what they are.

There must also be a sensible flow to the ideas. The links between one idea and the next should be made clear as the connection will be the link to reasons or might be a conclusion.

Here is an example to further illustrate the notion of reason. We need to be both reasonable; and reasoning if we want to think critically. Consider each situation and the information supplied on the two adjoining columns to distinguish between what is fair and what is logical.

You will notice that there is not always a clear distinction among all the statements as to what constitutes fair versus what is logical. Any statement can be perceived to be both fair and logical. Ricardo Semler, CEO of the highly successful Brazilian company SEMCO and author of *The Seven-Day Weekend*, asks some

Situation	Being reasonable *Asking: Is it a fair and a good thing?*	Being reasoning *Asking: Are the reasons logical and well connected?*
Should I speak out about my concerns in the workplace? Should there be democracy in the workplace?	I can speak out in many areas of life, e.g. at the bank, in the family, at school. It is a basic human right to participate in decision making.	Industrial democracy laws in Australia assert the requirement for consultation with workers. Ignoring workers may also be ignoring problems of productivity and efficiency. Lack of a voice may lead to sickness and stress and result in resource wastage.

Situation	Being reasonable	Being reasoning
	Asking: Is it a fair and a good thing?	*Asking: Are the reasons logical and well connected?*
Should I accept the new venture or job?	The earnings are lucrative. I possess skills to do the job. It is interesting. They seem like nice people to work for.	The work is challenging and highly engineered which fits my criteria for work. I am a premium player in the field required. The new venture will build my unique market niche. The work will improve my sustainability.

challenging questions which appeal to what is both reasonable and reasoning. He uses the powerful tool of contrast to point out the inconsistencies in our practices: Why are we able to answer emails on Sundays, but unable to go to the movies on Monday afternoon? Why can't we take the kids to work if we can take work home?

Asking whether the reasons given are good and fair is the first important step to critical thinking and it ensures the basic questions are asked. Basic questions are factual and descriptive rather than explanatory and they help ensure the essential meaning of the conversation is shared.

Exercise on 'reason'

Below are two situations. Jot down one or two statements that seem to be reasonable and reasoning about those situations. Invent a third situation of your own and note how you might be both reasonable and reasoning about it.

Situation	Being reasonable *Asking: Is it a fair and a good thing?*	Being reasoning *Asking: Are the reasons logical and well connected?*
1. As you walk along the street you notice two teenagers brawling. You ignore it.		
2. The receptionist asks the doctor to go buy some milk and goodies for morning tea.		
3.		

Assumptions

An assumption is something you know or at least think you know. It may be information that might be relevant and useful or it might not.

> *Thinking critically is the capacity to identify and challenge assumptions.*

The basis for bringing about change is to become critically reflective about our assumptions. While our thinking habits cause us to see the same patterns to make sense of the world—a necessary shortcut in some situations—we limit ourselves when we do not question how we give meaning to our experiences. By remaining fixed in our views, we are unable to respond to the changing environments around us.

What's an assumption?

An assumption is simply information or knowledge that you may or may not be aware you possess. The first step to becoming a critical thinker is to develop your capacity to know what you know and then to develop strategies to challenge what you know. When you question what you know or what is generally held to be true, you may discover something different. Here is an example:

> In a room with a locked door and a small open window there is a table, a bed, a chair and broken glass on the floor. Next to the glass Romeo and Juliet lie dead. How did they die?

Most people will probably think of the characters in Shakespeare's play and answer accordingly, but we haven't actually been told this. The answer to the riddle is that Romeo and Juliet are pet goldfish that died when their fish tank fell and smashed. The assumption we needed to question here is our cultural knowledge. We probably jumped to the conclusion that Romeo and Juliet were humans, but in this case that knowledge is not relevant and even misleading.

A critical thinker may not necessarily know the answer but will be able to generate alternative interpretations. To conclude your particular knowledge is not relevant for this problem you first have to identify it as an assumption. Once you recognise where the names Romeo and Juliet come from—Shakespeare's play—then you are in a position to ask yourself whether your knowledge will be helpful in solving the problem. If Romeo and Juliet aren't Shakespeare's characters, who are they? Indeed, are they human beings? Thinking about how the presence of broken glass might cause death might lead you to consider all types of alternatives. One of the greatest strengths in thinking critically is to question your own knowledge which you take for granted without realising that you take it for granted. What you know, perhaps what we all have always known and what we believe to be true, are the stumbling blocks of your critical thinking capacity.

Yogi Berra, the American baseball player, was a natural at

challenging assumptions as illustrated in his saying: 'When you come to a fork in the road, take it'. The humour challenges the accepted notion or conventional wisdom that when confronted with a choice you can only take one, not both. Humour results from being taken from one perspective to another perspective and then looking back, seeing the first perspective and realising that you have been subtly transported to where you are.

Now that you are beginning to challenge your long-held beliefs, you are starting to think critically.

Explicit and implicit assumptions

There are two basic types of assumptions: **explicit** and **implicit**. An explicit assumption is information stated in conversation.

Using an explicit assumption

> I think I might take my umbrella with me because I don't
> trust the weather forecast.

The explicit assumption here is information that is shared about not trusting the weather bureau. If the assumption was not made explicit you may *think* you know why the person is taking the umbrella but you will not be sure. You may think the weather forecast was for rain when in fact it was not.

An implicit, or tacit, assumption is information that is not stated in the conversation. When you make a statement you cannot say everything about that statement so you take it for granted that people understand the foundation of your statement and that you do not have to explain every detail. For example, when you refer to a cat, you implicitly assume your audience knows what a cat is. You cannot communicate without making assumptions. So making assumptions is not necessarily bad—it's part of effective communication. What is not helpful is if you take it for granted that everyone else understands your assumptions and fail to check they understand your meaning the way you intend it to be understood. If you want to send a clear message, leave nothing to chance!

Assumptions, then, are self-evident truths, unquestioned givens. Assumptions form the basis of your understanding of how the world works and how people behave. What you know intuitively influences how you interpret experience and the decisions you make.

Using an implicit assumption: the bus stop

If you meet a stranger at the bus stop and say, 'Good morning. Have you been waiting long?', you are assuming they can speak English, they are not deaf, they will respond to you, they are waiting to catch the bus etc.

All these and more are tacit assumptions. It would be a waste of time and pointless to state all the assumptions that exist and, besides, it would be impossible because they would only come from a single point of view—your own. Unstated personal information determines your perceptions, your decisions and your actions.

Every decision you make contains implicit assumptions. These assumptions usually restrict the solutions you will employ. Take, for example, the decision to start a business. You will assume that future revenue will be high enough in the long term to cover expenses and make a profit. You assume customers will purchase your services and products. You assume you can gain sufficient resources and support to make your business a success. You assume the staff you hire will deliver the service at the required standard. You expect your staff not to quit on the first day. Unless you identify and challenge these assumptions you may end up with unexpected results.

Three steps to identifying and challenging assumptions:
1. Identify a business decision (e.g. you want to increase your competitive advantage).
2. Identify the implicit (unstated) assumptions in this decision:
   - My competitors are taking business away from me.
   - I need to gain additional market share.
   - My strategy is effective.
   - My products and services are superior.
3. Challenge each assumption—an effective way to do this is to reverse each assumption.

- My competitors are not taking business away from me.
- I will not gain additional market share.
- My strategy will not be robust enough to deliver the edge.
- My products and services are inferior.

What effect do you think these challenges to your implicit assumptions will have on your decision? You may seek competitor analysis information and survey customers. You might be more careful and mindful in your approach and will strive for thoroughness—for example, plan, seek advice, pace yourself and avoid knee-jerk decisions. You may decide to abandon or postpone your decision until you are satisfied you have useful information that increases the likelihood of success against the odds.

You **identify** assumptions by probing for factual information by asking basic questions requiring recall only—for example, where do you work? How many employees are there? You can also **probe** by asking 'high order questions'. This means asking questions that require **justification** and **qualification**. These types of questions request people to express their opinions.

You **challenge** assumptions by also asking for justification and qualification as well as for **comparison**, for **cause–effect relationships**, for **new possibilities** and for **self-evaluation**. These are also high-order questions. The person you ask will have perceptions about the question and will choose particular aspects to comment on. Thus an opinion or feeling will be expressed. Any sort of question might be interpreted by the receiver as a challenge to their assumptions. The cultural and interpersonal contexts help to create the framework for challenge.

Identifying assumptions

Probing is an effective way of getting people to think more deeply about what they say. When you ask a probing question you get people to move beyond their first statement. You will be asking someone to respond immediately to your question, to give you an unrehearsed response to clarify what they just said. Examples of simple probing questions are:

- What do you mean by that?
- Can you tell me more about that?
- Can you give me an example of what you said?
- Can you say that again but use different words?
- Can you say that again but in a different sequence (for example, work backwards from the solution)?

The two means of probing are asking for a justification or a qualification. Asking for justification is a means of clarifying the reasons. Reasons are statements of comparison because they are linked to the original statement in a convincing way. Once the reasons are made explicit you are in a position to judge if they are reasonable (that is, good and fair). In asking for justification you are seeking to understand the basis for the statement, you are seeking a contrast. You want to know which assumptions do not apply to the original statement (that is, which assumptions do not link very well at all).

Justification

If you are not sure what someone is assuming, ask for a justification:

- What are your reasons for saying that?
- Can you give me any further explanation?

In using justification let's revisit the umbrella:

> I think I might take my umbrella with me because I don't trust the weather forecast.

When you ask the speaker to justify their decision, they might reply:

> I am assuming the weather forecast will continue to be unreliable. Also, if it is really hot and sunny I can still use my umbrella to shade myself!

Asking about assumptions is a useful way of identifying bias. However, a probing question like, 'What are you assuming?' may not be easy to answer. The person may not know what they are assuming and they may not know what their reasons are for saying what they do. They may not be able to tell you any more about their statement unless you probe more specifically. You can probe in a specific way by asking the person to qualify what they said.

Qualification

When you ask for qualification you're asking someone to identify the boundaries or limits of their statement. The way to do this is to ask for examples of when their statement *does not* apply. You are virtually asking them to build a fence around their statement and to give you an idea of what sort of things belong outside that fence and what additional things belong inside the fence.

For example, someone tells you that a worker is very lazy. When you ask the speaker to justify their statement, they reply:

> That person never helps to clean up. He always stands around talking to customers while everyone else does the work.

The question then becomes one of justification: 'Is talking to customers a behaviour that can be labelled as laziness?' But this question does not probe deeply enough. A question of qualification will clarify this even further.

> Are there times when talking to customers does *not* constitute laziness?

The answer might be, 'Yes, when customers are giving their orders, then it is appropriate to chat with them. But when they are not giving orders, employees should get on with the job required at that time.'

In this case, asking for a qualification illuminates the context and some work expectations.

Asking for qualification is asking for what is excluded and what is not relevant. Qualification provides information that is a contrast. The information shows differences. Examples of questions of qualification are:

- Is that always the case?
- Can you tell me when your statement would not apply?
- When else will your statement apply? Does it apply in this case?

In the umbrella example, use would be:

> I think I might take my umbrella with me because I don't
> trust the weather forecast.

Qualifying questions might include:

> 'Are there times when you *do* trust the forecast?'
> 'Are there times when you don't take your umbrella with you?'
> 'Would you take your umbrella with you if it was a mild
> spring day?'

Answers might include:

> I wouldn't take my umbrella if the forecast is for a fine day.
> I only take my umbrella when I hear an extreme forecast. This is
> because I don't trust extreme forecasts but I usually trust ordinary
> forecasts. So if it was a mild spring day and no extreme weather
> had been forecast, I would leave my umbrella home but I would
> still look at the sky before I left home without the umbrella.

Here's another example of probing to identify implicit assumptions by asking the person to qualify their meaning:

> John arrived late for work today so I gave him a written warning.

Asking for justification: 'What are your reasons for giving him a written warning (based on this incident)?'

> John is poor at punctuality and I'm annoyed that he was late
> today because we had some important work to do. Also, it was
> very inconvenient because my other staff member had to work
> past their finishing time until John arrived.

Some of the assumptions and reasons for the written warning identified in this statement include:

John arrives late on many occasions (poor at punctuality).
The boss gets annoyed.
There was important work to do.
Other staff members were inconvenienced (had to work past their finishing time).

Are these good reasons for giving a written warning? Many organisations have a policy on misconduct and the issuing of written warnings. A written policy known and agreed to by staff creates an environment of fairness when the policy is implemented consistently and properly. If all four reasons given for the written warning are contained in the policy, then we might judge them as good reasons. On the other hand, we might question the appropriateness of some of them being in a policy. Also, we might ask if the boss usually gives a written warning when annoyed? So you would then ask for qualification.

In relation to lateness, when would you *not* issue a written warning?
If it was the first time John was late or if there was nothing important to be done, I would not have given John the written warning.

This technique clarifies the boss's initial statement. It has become clear that there are two key criteria for the boss's actions. Even though the boss stated other reasons, in the end the written warning is issued for only two conditions, that there has been a previous warning and that important work was in need of being done.

Of course, we don't actually know what the written policy says. We might probe further with basic questions to identify the points in the written policy. We might also press further to determine if just one reason is robust enough to issue the written warning. We might then come to the conclusion that only one reason is required for a written warning and that there has been at least one previous warning issued. Strictly speaking, the other reasons did not trigger the written warning action.

Challenging assumptions

High-order questions are key tools for challenging assumptions. Your purpose is not to criticise but to invite the other person to test the fairness and relevance of the information given. High-order questions are not questions of fact but questions about *opinion, beliefs* and *feelings*. Therefore, there is no right or wrong answer. For best effect, always challenge in a collegial way, taking care not to threaten or come across as supercilious. You can challenge by asking for **comparison**, for **cause–effect relationships**, for **new possibilities** and for **self-evaluation**.

Comparisons

Asking for a comparison means asking about two different things, like apples and oranges. How are they the same? They are both fruit. They both have skin or peel. They both have pips. The both grow on trees etc. A comparison asks how two or more things are the *same*.

It is more challenging to focus on similarity rather than on difference. Surprisingly, when you focus on similarity the differences jump out at you! This focus on similarity will help you to reconsider the value of your assumptions.

The simplest comparison asks whether two or more things in the same group are *identical*, for example:

Question: Is a mussel the same thing as a clam?
Answer: _____

The next comparison tests the degree of similarity so that you can identify what they have in common:

Question: How are a tree and a sheet of paper the same?
Answer: _____

A more complex comparison is to ask people to relate sets of ideas or similar points:

Question: How is the life cycle of a bumble bee similar to that
of an ant?
Answer: _____

The most challenging comparison is to choose which aspects
you want to compare between two seemingly abstract items:

Question: How are democracy and communism the same?
Answer: _____

Another way to ask this question is to say: What are democracy
and communism an example of? Test yourself on this comparison.

Question: How is asking for comparisons like asking for
qualification? (What are asking for comparisons and asking
for qualifications an example of?)

Possible answer: They are both sorting processes.

In all cases you are creating categories. You want to know if two
things belong in the same category. What is in this category and
what is out? Apples and oranges are fruit. They belong in the same
category. Comparison and qualification are both sorting and
affirming activities. The important thing is not to try for absolute
accuracy and not to get into an argument! Remember that there
are no two things in the world so different that they cannot be
compared.

The aim of comparison is to stimulate thinking about the
assumption and to allow the challenge to present itself. Your goal is
not to exaggerate the importance of the similarities and not to over-
value the importance of the differences. What should happen is that
you think about the assumption more carefully. In doing so, you
have challenged the assumption.

To use comparison let's look at the umbrella example again:

I think I might take my umbrella with me because I don't
trust the weather forecast.

What common elements do these two assumptions have? Is trusting the weather forecast the same as trusting the government's economic forecast? What common elements do these two assumptions have? Is trusting the weather forecast the same as trusting a friend, a colleague, your boss, a government representative, your family? A question of comparison is a way of exploring an issue that uncovers and challenges many assumptions. When you ask for comparison you are really asking the person to suggest a higher category in which the things being compared will fit. This is difficult because it requires the person to think at a higher level of abstraction than is presented by the things being compared.

Cause–effect relationships

You cannot observe causal relationships directly though you may guess that one thing causes another. In many cases the cause remains hidden for long after the effect has been seen. You can often get it wrong. When things happen together it is easy to mistakenly think that one is causing the other. When you see one thing happen just before another it is also easy to think that the first thing caused the second. There are many mysteries in life, but you should not hold back from trying to understand them to improve the situation.

Your aim is to find links that connect with each other. There will be links between events, people, objects or ideas. Again, the aim is not to prove conclusively that one thing causes another, but to think more deeply about causal relationships. Adopting a tentative or 'temporary' approach is useful. The following questions will help you to uncover cause–effect relationships.

- Does one idea or event cause the other? What is the seemingly obvious impact?
- Are both events a result of something else?
- Because one thing happened first, does that mean it caused it?
- Does this event fully explain why the other is happening?
- What else might be contributing to this situation?
- Does this chain of events mean that one always leads to the other?

The umbrella example in a causal reasoning would go:

> I think I might take my umbrella with me because I don't
> trust the weather forecast.

Does hearing the weather forecast cause the person to take their umbrella with them? Are the weather forecast and the person taking their umbrella with them the result of something else? Does the weather forecast fully explain why the person takes their umbrella with them?

We pride ourselves in being rational, logical thinkers. Perhaps we have become creatures of linear thinking or categorical thinking (that is, we think and live in categories). If we think like this, things are either good or bad, not both good and bad; true or false, not both. A thing cannot be itself and its opposite at the same time, yet we catch ourselves saying, 'yes and no', at times or that a particular thing can be 'both'. And we have expressions like 'less is more', 'living is dying' and 'hating is loving'! Opposites can be more related than we thought at first glance. They co-exist and even improve each other. Here is an example of a mysterious cause–effect.

You often hear these days about acrimonious divorces. The question that pops into your mind is, 'What happened?'. The answer is often, 'He cheated on her'. Does the cheating fully explain the acrimonious break-up? Probably not. Perhaps she loved him too much. She was certainly very hurt. The more you love a person the more you can hate them. Love can lead to hate. In fact, love and hate can even enhance each other. In some marriages there are many moments when they co-exist, when they are actually indistinguishable. So an acrimonious divorce is an incredibly complex scenario to try to fathom. What you can do is to examine what you know about the two people involved and accept that opposites can co-exist.

Workers seem to participate more in the workplace these days. What caused that? Perhaps it is participative approaches where there are now processes of consultation and workers are asked to say what they think. There are committees established where workers can identify problems and suggest solutions to improve the workplace.

These reasons seem plausible. But it is also true that many workers are sceptical. Some maintain that participative approaches are a mild form of domination. Here is one worker's statement about democracy in the workplace that shows that things are more complex than they first seem:

> The executives have not really given up any of their authority. They put us in teams so they can get what they want. They want us to work harder, which we do. When it counts they still have the power and authority and do not listen to us if it does not suit them. We do not really have a democratic workplace where it counts. The point is that the executives seem to have given us authority but they have not given us any of *their* authority. They do not have less even though it seems we have more.

So we see that some workers will say that participative work practices have caused increased democracy in the workplace while others maintain that these practices are simply a cause of a more surreptitious type of domination by the executive. Asking the 'cause–effect' question as a means of probing will uncover many implicit assumptions. We have not proved anything; however, we have uncovered points of view of great value that have led to a deeper appreciation of the situation.

New possibilities

When we ask others for new possibilities we are asking them to enjoy ambiguity, to find different paths, to play with the ideas, to take risks, to think laterally. Generating options is a very important step to thinking critically. This is because people often have one of two reactions to a situation or idea. When they first hear an idea they will probably decide immediately if they like it or don't. Just as when you first hear about a problem you will immediately have an answer or you will have no idea about a solution. Perhaps you carry around in your head an assumption, a personal belief that problems usually have one best solution. If you have no idea about a solution you will be striving to think of a single solution rather than aiming to generate a number of options.

This is a feeling we all need to learn to let go of. We need to avoid the compulsion to quickly resolve on one answer. Learn to enjoy ambiguity. Learn to love lack of resolution. Welcome the cacophony of modern symphonic sounds. Make a shift from our taste for resolution, to seeking asymmetry. We need to welcome ambiguity and make it our natural state instead of submitting to the common strain of forming opinions that will fit everything into a harmonious and comfortable picture.

The critical thinking process demands that we try to suspend our judgement about an idea and create new possibilities. It demands that we will not be satisfied with a single solution even if it looks like the perfect solution. It requires us to be happily welcoming of asymmetry and seeking of ambiguity. Trying to think of more options is fundamental to the critical thinking process. This means that we won't be looking for symmetry in the patterns of thought but enjoying asymmetries.

As an example of new possibilities, a man runs towards home as fast as he can. When he gets there, there is a man wearing a mask. Ask yourself what images came into your head when you read this statement.

- Did you envisage a man wearing a suit or casual clothes or sports clothes?
- Did you imagine a man running along a footpath, on the road, in the country or on a sports field?
- Did you imagine a real man or a plastic object such as a token on a Monopoly game?
- What sort of home was he running to—was it a dwelling in suburbia, a country home or a retirement institution or home on a board game or in a real game?
- What sort of mask was the man wearing—was it a party mask, a fireman's mask or a sports mask such as a baseball mask?

It is likely that your first reaction will be related to what you most commonly experience. Your answers to the questions above might include:

- The man ran home where he found a surprise party waiting for him, and some of the guests were wearing masks.
- When he arrived home, the man found a fireman in a mask extinguishing a fire at his house.
- When the man arrived home he put on a mask because he is a different person at home compared to when he is away from home.

All of the solutions in the above example are conceptual leaps that involve both divergent and convergent thinking. Convergent thinking occurs when you ask yourself what your actual thoughts are about the situation based on your current knowledge and explicit assumptions. That is, your thoughts 'converge' on your specific existing knowledge and experience. The sequence of your experience establishes a main pattern or path of perception that actually maintains a neutral course if a satisfactory solution eludes you. The dominance of convergent thinking along the main path prevents any alternative path or perceptual pattern from emerging. It is only natural for the brain to abhor chaos and to seek resolution and symmetry. You most probably have symmetrical thought patterns on the narrative of the story up until a different idea switches your perception.

Divergent thinking occurs when you have that different idea, when you think 'outside the box' and consider possibilities other than your strict knowledge and assumptions about past situations. Divergent thinking is the same as lateral thinking, where you move beyond the obvious and logical that is immediately transparent to you. You move your thinking obliquely onto a more abundant side path.

Another lateral solution is that the man running home was playing baseball and when he runs home there is the keeper with the mask waiting for him to get him out. Playing this game in a group would demonstrate how many different possibilities there are to thinking about an issue or problem. Can you create more options to the example above of the man running home?

When we ask for new possibilities we are identifying and challenging assumptions. By creating new possibilities we are also inventing new assumptions and new scenarios that lead to creativity. We can only achieve this if we have an attitude of loving ambiguity.

Self-evaluation

When asking for self-evaluation to probe further, you tend to ask a reflexive question. A reflexive question is one that focuses on what a person thinks, feels and does about herself or himself. It's a question that asks you to judge the worth of your own thoughts, feelings and actions. It's a challenge that will lead to a greater awareness of the way you think and feel. A reflexive question gives you an opportunity to reflect on your current perceptions and habits and to consider changing these.

Reflexive questions include:

- What is my usual way of thinking about problems?
- How do my feelings affect the way I think and make decisions?
- Would it be useful for me to improve my ability to learn from my actions?
- What do my colleagues think about the way I solve problems?

Using reflexive questioning in the umbrella example would read:

> I think I might take my umbrella with me because I don't trust the weather forecast.

Ask these reflexive questions to probe further:

- What do you think about yourself thinking in this way?
- Why do you think this way?
- Do you use this pattern of thinking in other areas of your life?
- If you keep thinking in this way, will it affect the kind of person you are and will it affect you in the future?
- Have you learned anything about yourself by discussing how you think?

For example, with the weather bureau, was the forecast only hot and sunny without a mention of possible showers? Will the umbrella be used to shade from the hot sun rather than simply protecting from rain that you expect?

Reflexive questions are designed to raise your own cognitive awareness. This means you will understand better the way you think and hopefully this will lead to greater personal control and effectiveness. The assumption that knowing how you think makes you a better thinker could be an erroneous assumption. Does knowing how you are a friend make you a better friend? Does knowing how you raise your children make you a better mother or father? Does knowing how you lead make you a better leader? Reflection on our current habits is a strong basis for improvement.

Let me explain the importance of reflecting on our habits this way by asking you to imagine a roll of barbed wire. When you look at it there is no problem identifying it for what it is and the function it has—usually a preventative one to keep enemies out. Pretty well any spot on the wire will have the same effect. There are just never-ending twirls of wire with innumerable protruding razor-sharp spikes. It is difficult to know where the wire and spikes begin and where they end. This image is not a pleasant one and may conjure up images of war and suffering. The wire represents a stream of entwined consciousness and unconsciousness where one is indistinguishable from the other. The spikes represent a stream of entwined competence and incompetence where one is indistinguishable from the other. This image is a metaphor for attainment of expertise such as thinking critically.

Think of a staircase with five steps and these words written on each step in this order from the top step down:

- Conscious unconscious competence
- Unconscious competence
- Conscious competence
- Conscious incompetence
- Unconscious incompetence.

Life begins with the bottom step (unconscious incompetence) because we are born without an awareness or competence for survival—we are totally dependent. Gradually, with development, a child becomes aware of its incapacity to feed itself (conscious incompetence) and then starts to do something about it, striving to achieve the basics (conscious competence). Finally, children become so expert they are not aware of how they do routine things (unconscious competence). The mark of an expert and professional is that they are aware of their skills and performance while performing. They can think about how they are thinking while they are actually thinking. This is the highest level of being conscious of your unconscious competence.

We might say that a baby is born with a level of unconscious incompetence. It doesn't know it can't feed itself and survive without help. We might say that a manager is viewed by the staff as being unconsciously incompetent because he or she is not aware of the number of continual blunders and catastrophic decisions he or she makes. Of course, the manager does not hold the same view. He or she thinks that they have a high level of unconscious competence. They can do their job without having to think about it because they are expert at managing. The difference between unconscious incompetence and unconscious competence is a matter of interpretation or perception. If one can be mistaken for the other it would appear there is a seamless connection like the strand of barbed wire.

A similar situation exists with the notions of conscious competence and unconscious competence. Staff think the boss knows exactly what she is doing because she is so good at it. But the boss maintains that she is not really aware of how she gets such good results because it comes naturally without even having to think about it. If we are not comfortable with ambiguity, with multiple resolutions and interpretations we might view life as barbed wire where we are always trying to extricate ourselves from wrong perceptions to avoid the pain of continual self-improvement. People who relish ambiguity will not feel the pain of the barbed wire. They will enjoy the thrill of upgrading their habits. They will see it as vital to the joy of living.

If you know someone who is a leader—for example, a CEO or a person you consider is doing a great job and truly demonstrating leadership—ask them a reflexive question such as: 'What things make you the sort of leader you are?' Some of the responses you receive may be quite banal. Some people cannot always articulate clearly the criteria that makes them great leaders. Even though they are effective in what they do, nevertheless they may understand very little about what distinguishes their performance. If this is the case, should we conclude that increasing awareness of ourselves is not necessary? Perhaps we should avoid the reflexive questions and just get on with the job! Navel gazing can be a waste of time. Effective critical thinkers by their nature relish reflexive questions and pursuits. They're inclined towards internal ambiguity and so are always on the quest for different shades of themselves.

These are some of the qualities great leaders have, which they may or may not know they possess:

- They understand the context in which they make their decisions.
- They have a useful perspective for viewing human affairs and they can distinguish what is important to people.
- They can show people the way to achieve a vision; they can encourage people to strive for a goal.
- They have ability, affability and availability.
- Where it counts they have clout, competence and compatibility, the capacity to get along with others.
- They search for opportunities and embrace failure as an opportunity to learn and grow.
- They are able to build teams with spirit and cohesion and can inspire courage and hope.

In this section on assumptions I have explored in various ways how a focus on what we know, whether we are conscious of it or not, is vital to our capacity to think critically. Knowledge is the most powerful force in our thinking and a lot of it is hidden from others and ourselves. Knowledge and the experience that is inextricably bound to it acts like the water, wind and gravity—eroding on our thinking, carving the rivers, gullies and pathways in our reasoning. The shaping of our thinking is achieved in the formative years of our lives but it should not stop there.

The shaping of a river takes centuries and so changing its course is a formidable task. In fact a river never stops changing. It is difficult to identify assumptions that underlie people's values and behaviours. Assumptions that underpin people's actions and behaviours act as reasons for those behaviours. When the reasons are identified then we can judge how fair and reasonable those assumptions are. More importantly we can question those reasons. Questioning leads to creating different points of view and possibly learning from them. Learning is the mechanism that changes our rivers and pathways.

Perspectives

It is not possible to create a fresh viewpoint without thinking critically. Albert Einstein said that you cannot solve a problem from the same perspective that created it. When you engage in reasoning and challenge your own assumptions you may reflect deeply enough to create a new outlook. This means you will arrive at a fresh understanding and appreciation of the issue. Fresh perspectives enable you to develop fully as a person and to contribute significantly to your workplace and to a democratic society.

The challenge then is to learn how to create a fresh perspective, a new viewpoint. One approach is to identify and challenge the relevance of assumptions. It will be necessary to suspend some tacit assumptions of your original perspective of defining and understanding the problem. A second approach is to engage in re-framing.

Re-framing is thinking sideways. It means breaking away from orthodox ideas and practices and creating ideas with a different velocity. Here is a story to illustrate how everyday thinking is re-framed by a punch line which introduces an understanding with a different force. What is revealed is a different perspective. Only in hindsight can we appreciate the difference. Of course, the person with the different perspective acts on it from the start but cannot always reveal it or wish to reveal it.

The story is about a teenager travelling on a Melbourne tram with his friends when the inspector boards the tram and asks everyone for their tickets. Everyone produces their ticket except for the teenager who frantically starts searching everywhere for it—in all his pockets, his wallet, his bag. He is so flustered and almost flamboyant to everyone's entertainment because they can see he has the ticket in his mouth the whole of the time. Unable to suffer this fool any longer the inspector grabs the ticket from the teenager's mouth, punches it and returns it to his mouth, muttering something that acknowledges the teenager's apparent foolishness! Once the inspector has left the tram his friends continue laughing and ask him if he didn't feel an utter idiot all that time looking for his ticket when it was right there in his mouth. The teenager replies that he didn't feel a fool one bit: 'I was slowly chewing off the date'.

The same methods to identify and challenge the relevance of assumptions apply to creating new perspectives—this can be a protracted exploration to uncover assumptions that might be faulty or that can be discarded. Thinking critically is not a magic bullet that produces solutions after minor exploration. Here is a detailed example to illustrate how new perspectives can be created.

You may have heard the brainteaser about the farmer who has to cross the river with his fox, chicken and a box of grain in order to get to market. He has a very small boat that will sink if he carries more than one item across the river at a time. The problem is that if he takes the fox, the chicken will eat the grain. If he takes the grain, the fox will eat the chicken. Logic might prompt the farmer to take the chicken across the river first so that the fox and the grain can be left safely behind for a later trip, but this will give him a problem on the second trip. If he takes the fox, it will eat the chicken while he is returning to collect the grain. If he takes the grain, the chicken will eat the grain while he is returning to collect the fox.

Ask for comparisons

Question: Is the problem of getting the animals and the grain across the river the same as getting them across dry land?

Answers: The farmer must keep the fox from eating the chicken and the chicken from eating the grain. You will have a means of transportation in both cases. In both cases there is a beginning of the trip and an end.

You may think that transporting them across dry land wouldn't require several journeys because the means of transport is different; for example, boat versus cart—on land it may only be one trip whereas on water the restrictions clearly dictate more than one trip. To think this way is to focus on difference and contrast rather than similarity and comparison. It is not always easy to think of comparisons because it is the contrasts that tend to jump out at us. We are exploring and trying to increase awareness and possibility of challenging assumptions. This will lead to new perspectives simply because we are introducing new (random) elements for comparison. If new differences pop up, then that is well and good because there will be opportunity to identify new perspectives and hence solutions.

> Question: How is travel by boat the same as travel by cart, by foot, by horse?

> Answer: The animals still must be protected from each other.

They must be supervised. Whatever the vehicle, it must be controlled and directed. The animals and grain need to fit into the means of transport either all together or in combination or singly.

> Question: How is transporting these items across the river safely the same as getting three different items across the river safely?

> Answer: The weight of each item must be under a tolerable limit.

> Question: Is the chicken/fox/grain transportation problem the same as transporting three people called Geoff, Fred and Charles—if left alone, would Fred kill Charles, would Charles kill Fred and would Geoff be safe only from Fred?

> Answer: _____

From the exploration above we know the farmer can travel safely with all three items, although not necessarily with all three together. He can still only transport one at a time on the boat. So, have any new assumptions arisen that you feel should be discarded to give you a different perspective that might lead to a punch line, a solution that fits the requirements? If not, try other approaches.

Ask for cause–effect relationships

Question: Does one idea or event cause the other?

Answer: No. We might argue that their respective places on the food chain causes the fox to eat the chicken and the chicken to eat the grain. It is the natural order of things—instinct. Somehow the farmer must keep the chicken and fox away from each other and the chicken away from the grain while he is with them, but he cannot supervise their activities when they are alone.

Question: Are both events a result of something else? In other words, is the fact of being left alone and the result of one eating the other the cause of something else?

Answer: Both could be a result of the animals not being restrained or prevented by other means of interacting with each other. For example, the fox could be tied on a leash so it cannot reach the chicken, and the grain could be stored in a way that is inaccessible to the chicken—for example, a tight lid to seal the grain container.

Question: Because one event happens first, does that mean it causes an event that follows?

Answer: No, the farmer leaving with the grain does not cause the fox to eat the chicken. Normally, foxes eat chickens if they find them and can have access to them. Chickens eat grain if it is within their reach. This seems to be dictated by their natural drive for survival.

Question: Does this chain of events mean that one always leads to the other?

Answer: Not if the animals are restrained. Not if the animals are transported in isolation and a critical pair is not left alone.

Question: What else might be contributing to this situation?

Answer: Leaving easy access to each other contributes to the situation.

Ask for new possibilities

Probing for possibilities is a way of checking out the rules of the story and the fine details of the scenario. For example:

- Can the context be changed?
- Does the market run along the river bank opposite the farmer's house and if so can he leave the chicken locked up while he takes the grain across the river first and then the fox before he comes back for the chicken?
- If the river is not next to the farm how does the farmer get them there?
- How are the chicken and fox transported? Do they walk on a leash or are they in their own boxes?
- Is there only one person in the story? Does the farmer have a son or daughter or someone who can look after the chicken and fox while he transports the grain first and then the fox? (This is a childlike fishing for information to break the restrictions of the story. It's a type of thinking aloud exploration.)
- Can the farmer take the chicken to market on a different day?

Ask for self-evaluation

- What is my usual way of thinking about problems?
- How am I thinking about this problem?
- How do my feelings affect the way I think and make decisions?
- How do I feel about this particular problem?

- How can I improve my ability to think by being more aware of how I think about this problem or other problems?

The above questioning process may lead to a solution. It may lead to fresh insights and a new perspective. One answer might be: if the chicken was in a lightweight high-security cage safe from the fox and unable to access the grain when left alone with it, then the problem would be easily solved. Another solution to this problem is revealed later in this chapter that discusses the skill of re-framing.

Framing and re-framing

> Wisdom is not the same as cleverness . . .
> Wisdom is not a function of intelligence . . .
> Wisdom is more about perspective than detail . . .
> Cleverness is like having a library full of books.
> Wisdom is knowing which book to read at the moment.
> —Edward de Bono, psychologist and author

Perspective is about openness: open your mind! I maintain that the chief characteristic of thinking critically is 'openness'. This capacity for openness serves us well when we want to question ideas or search for difference. Fundamentally, openness is a disposition for thinking critically and creatively. We know we will have adopted an attitude of openness when we have disintegrated our unwillingness to respect the views of others and tendency to ignore alternative frames. Edward de Bono maintains that wisdom is more about perspective than detail. In this sense wisdom, deciding on the right perspective, is fundamental to thinking critically and creatively. An important tool of openness is the procedure of framing and re-framing. Framing and re-framing are about perspective.

Take a picture and place it in a simple wooden frame and you experience a particular effect. Now replace the wooden frame with a well-embellished, very large and chunky gold frame that is twice the size, weight, colour and effect of the first frame. When you re-frame the same picture you bring out different aspects of a scenario.

Humour results from re-framing, from being transported from one perspective to another perspective and then seeing the first frame and realising you have been subtly transported to where you are. This is the basis for thinking creatively and critically—changing the frame, looking back and smiling because you realise the subtle yet powerful displacement. For example, notice the powerful displacement in Samuel Goldwyn's words: 'I don't pay any attention to him. I don't even ignore him.' He very powerfully points out a new perspective of the nature of 'ignoring', which is to pay attention. The irony brings laughter. This is poetic—a powerful way of being critically reflective. I think humour makes us innately human because it is the basis of our thinking modus-operandi.

Another aspect of the power of reframing is that it brings insight: suddenly viewing something in a novel way and noticing the link back to the original frame. Re-framing is a skill of deliberate insight while sleeping on it and hoping your gut feeling will emerge is a hit-and-miss attitude towards insight.

Of all the dimensions of critical thinking, 'openness' is the hub or central skill from which others emanate. In essence, re-framing is best practised in a group at the hub of the spinning hourglass. Re-framing is the skill of interpreting and being open to a situation from a different point of view. It is a special technique that helps us tune our understanding and feelings to a situation. Re-framing is a creative technique that suggests options for thinking, feeling and acting. Re-framing includes objective re-framing and subjective re-framing. Objective and subjective re-framing are two ways of becoming critically aware because you view the same scenario from two different perspectives.

There is a story told of an Australian five-year-old boy, Johnny, who was constantly teased by his mates. They asked him to choose one of two Australian coins to keep, either the $1 coin or the $2 coin. Johnny fancied the bigger one so he took the $1 coin. At that moment his mates made him the laughing stock for choosing the one worth only half the value of the other. 'What a moron he is for choosing the lesser amount', they laughed and mocked. Many times they used Johnny as the laughing stock by playing this joke on him. One day his parents told Johnny that if teased again he should take the smaller $2 coin, which is twice the value of the bigger coin he was always choosing. This was sure to stop the teasing. 'But', Johnny replied to his parents, 'if I did that I would never have collected so many $1 gold coins'.

Re-framing is thinking laterally. It means escaping from accepted ideas and practices and creating ideas of a different momentum. Re-framing is a skill that can be applied by individuals on their own or in groups.

Objective re-framing

If you are listening to a conversation and you question the speaker about his assumptions, you are questioning assumptions outside yourself. Asking a speaker or an outsider about their assumptions is the first step to re-framing. The second step is being open to those assumptions. It is not enough to just identify the assumptions; you then have to be open to them.

Let's reconsider the story about the farmer going to market with the grain, the chicken and the fox which I talked about earlier in this chapter. There seems to be an assumption by the author of this story that the problem has a solution or trick to it but it nevertheless has an answer. That is, we might imagine the author has created a tricky problem that requires a twist in thinking to get the answer and once we have the solution we will see it was so simple and obvious that we feel silly to have missed it! This awareness of possible assumptions by the author should energise us and lead us to think of simple and perhaps more obvious solutions.

If we could access the author we might ask them directly about their assumptions. This would be a productive move. They might say they genuinely do not know if there is a solution. We can still engage in objective re-framing if we ask other people what they think the assumptions about the problem might be. This might uncover some interesting ideas to consider.

When someone tells you about a work problem they frame it in a particular way that shows their understanding of the problem. Sometimes a problem is told (framed) in a way that contains a solution. Other times the way someone describes the problem will have no hint of any solution. You might imagine one but it won't be in the statement. Do you think it helps or hinders to describe a problem in a way that contains a solution? It may be better than not having any solution but in most cases a single solution will limit exploration of possibilities, even if you do end up with that solution.

Think about this question: 'I have no money in my pocket so how can I go to the movies?' This problem restricts you because the words 'how can I go to the movies?' leads to a solution that immediately points to having money in your pocket. Other possibilities such as using a credit card, asking a friend to help or a visit to the ATM may be overlooked. A better way to state this problem might be: 'What can I do to go to the movies?' The benefit of this type of problem statement, which does not hint at a solution, is that it might encourage people to search for a wide range of options.

How a problem is framed—the four Ps

The focus of objectively framing a problem is on fact rather than opinion and on cause rather than symptom. A single solution or assumption about a problem may point to opinion rather than fact. For example, 'employees consistently come late to meetings'. Late attendance at meetings may be the basic cause of the problem or it may be only a symptom of a deeper problem. The deeper problem could be low morale, inadequate conditions, the boss's consistent late arrival, stress in the workplace or something else.

Objective framing of a problem requires searching for broad information to pinpoint others' views of all the underlying causes. If you refuse to treat problems as simple things you will then be on the search for complexity and increase your chances of identifying causes rather than symptoms. Objective re-framing means taking into account many different points of view—not your own single view but others' views.

It is important to identify some of the fundamental causes for an effective focus on solutions to occur. If solutions are proposed that only focus on eliminating symptoms, the likely outcome might be an exacerbation of the problem. For example, poor time management has many causes, one of which is an inability to identify and prioritise goals and objectives. The solution of teaching time management techniques to employees will fail if it ignores a key cause as being the failure to identify and prioritise objectives. Employees might become more efficient but they will be doing the wrong things. Doing the wrong things faster can be catastrophic to any business!

When in doubt treat all problem statements as containing symptoms (assumptions) rather than causes and search for more information. Think of the four Ps of causes: people, policies, procedures, plant.

Subjective re-framing

Subjective re-framing occurs when you become critically reflective of your own assumptions, of your own frame of reference, your own thinking and where it came from and how you got your habit of thinking that way. This is a most powerful learning experience. It is very empowering when you question the assumptions that you have been taking for granted.

The challenge is to identify (describe) the frame you have placed around the scenario. There will be at least one element of your description of the way you frame the problem or issue that you have taken for granted. The method is to identify your own implicit assumptions and challenge them. Let us revisit an earlier example to search for an elegant solution by identifying and challenging your frame, a hidden assumption—the farmer going to market with the grain, the chicken and the fox.

There is at least one unstated assumption that seems logical in this scenario, but unless it is identified, challenged and rejected the problem cannot be viewed from a fresh perspective. It seems reasonable to think that once you take one item across the river you should not bring it back since the aim is to get everything across. Why is this a difficult assumption to identify? It is so obvious yet we take it so much for granted in the way others frame the problem originally.

Let us suppose the farmer takes the chicken across the river first, leaving the fox safely with the grain. The farmer comes back for the next one but is left with a dilemma. If he takes the fox across and then comes back for the grain, the fox will eat the chicken in his absence. If he takes the grain across and then comes back for the fox, the chicken will eat the grain in his absence. It is at this point of breakdown that the implicit assumption needs to be identified. A hidden assumption stands in the way of an elegant solution.

The unstated assumption is that taking any item *back* across the river on a return journey to the point of origin is hardly an option. The reason it is such a strong and hidden assumption is that it is integral to the goal the farmer has of getting everything safely across the river. To take anything back seems inefficient, ineffective and contradictory to achieving the goal. Without challenging this assumption such an elegant solution would not appear. Einstein's helpful hint, that you cannot solve a problem from the same perspective (framework of wisdom) that created the problem, seems appropriate. You should not be too severe on trying to achieve your goal strictly without giving a return joy ride to either the chicken or the fox

The only option it seems the farmer has is to take the chicken across the river first so that the fox is left with the grain. The farmer comes back and collects either the fox or the grain, it does not matter which because when he leaves, say, the fox on the other side he immediately takes the chicken with him on the return journey to collect the grain. He leaves the chicken alone and takes the grain across the river to leave with the fox, before returning and collecting the chicken for another joy ride!

This is not the only solution available to the farmer. Obviously, you may have detected other possibilities emanating from all the questioning and reflection you've done on this problem. We should not forget that there is no simple formula for solving problems. There is no guarantee that thinking critically will give us satisfactory answers. However, we can be sure that we will be able to challenge, explore and create new possibilities available to us.

Sue Vardon and Centrelink

Sue Vardon was the chief executive of the Department of Correctional Services in South Australia. In this position she introduced substantial reform of the correctional services system, reducing costs, developing a new corporate culture and a new management ethos based on improving customer service. In 1995 Sue was awarded the Inaugural Telstra Business Woman of the Year award. Subsequently she became the first CEO of Centrelink.

The Australian public as a whole have been frustrated by the fact that in order to obtain government assistance it was necessary for people to go to several government departments. The time was ripe for a radical approach for the delivery of government referral and payment services. It was time to 're-frame'. Reduce the many to a 'one-stop shop'! The Australian government decided to create a new statutory authority serving many government departments and providing a central point of service.

Centrelink combined the activities of the Department of Social Security and the Department of Education, Employment, Training and Youth Affairs. In combining the services people could obtain assistance from a central location that would have previously been received by going to a number of different departments. When launching Centrelink in 1997, Prime Minister John Howard described the creation of Centrelink as 'probably the biggest single reform undertaken in the area of service delivery during the last fifty years'.

Centrelink's services are provided under a purchaser/provider arrangement on behalf of over 23 different agencies across three levels of government. To give an idea of the breadth of the business, at the end of the millennium Centrelink had:

- 1000 points of service delivery, including 26 Call Centres
- 24 000 staff
- 6.4 million customers
- 70 different products and services
- 232 million payments each year ($47 billion)
- 100 million letters sent to customers

- 6.5 million home visits to customers
- 20 million office appointments
- 28.9 million website hits.

Centrelink is the first Australian organisation to declare it was on the path to becoming a learning organisation to develop leaders and a learning culture. This means that its competitive advantage would primarily depend on the knowledge and ability of its people and the application of that knowledge and ability to their jobs.

Centrelink has a range of ways in which it engages with citizens and encourages critical thinking to ensure people's feedback impacts on the way it does business. Value creation workshops are conducted in a similar way to focus groups—participants are selected from the relevant sector of the community. Centrelink has an annual survey program that collects people's perceptions of Centrelink. The results of surveys are disseminated to all customer service centres to act on. The surveys help to evaluate specific areas of Centrelink, customer service and identify areas for service improvement. Centrelink also works closely with many community groups listening and helping clients to understand each others' businesses and cooperate to get the best outcomes for people being helped. In these ways, Centrelink contributes to community building and social capital. Centrelink also has in place a range of consultative forums that enable the community to provide feedback and advice on all aspects of service delivery to customers. Sue Vardon says that Centrelink has a complex governance arrangement but it is the price for removing the complexity from the citizen. To achieve accurate information accessible to the citizen, Centrelink has to operate on the principle that the citizen can find services to help in their transition through an event in their lives at the one place, wherever that is. Centrelink's absolute responsibility is to shake out the murkiness of old governance arrangements, jealousies, tradition, excessive processes, silos and conflicting purposes at all levels of government and shine a light on them.

Sue Vardon also says that Centrelink needs to take the complexity (bureaucratic spaghetti) from in front of the counter to behind it and untangle it. She calls this governance drag back.

You may have got the idea in reading this book that what I am saying is that thinking critically is a rigorous and serious thing to do; that you have to be logical, asking the right questions, identifying the hard-to-find assumptions, challenging what others say and always trying to look at things in a different way. Well, yes, you are right. But if you find it all a bit much, too difficult to remember and to do then it is quite easy to make it all a bit simpler. Get yourself a mentor, someone like Sue Vardon, and collect some other practical ideas. If all else fails, take on a dream-like quality in your approach. Let your imagination relax, sway and run wild; allow the images to flow freely in your being and invite different hues into your thoughts. Perhaps this quote from Lewis Carroll will help you appreciate a little more how to be different. Turn your nightmares into dreams. Adventure through your thinking.

> In a Wonderland we lie,
> Dreaming as the days go by,
> Dreaming as the summers die:
> Ever drifting down the stream
> Lingering in the golden gleam
> Life, what is it but a dream?
> —Lewis Carroll, author

Exercises

Solution-framed problems

Study the following table. The first column contains problem statements. Next to each problem statement is a space to identify the solution suggested in the problem statements. You will notice that these framed-solutions are really assumptions contained in the way the problem is put in the first place. The first problem statement indicates that the load needs a larger vehicle to move it. This information stated in this way is an explicit assumption. It needs to be challenged. The third column contains space to list the challenges; that is, other possible solutions.

Thinking critically requires that when you describe a problem, you avoid defining the problem as a single disguised solution. Re-state each problem so it does not contain a solution in the problem statement. The first two have been done for you.

Problem statement	The framed solution (the assumption)	Alternative solutions (challenges)
Because the load is too heavy we will have to find a larger vehicle to transport it. *Re-state problem:* What options do we have to transport this heavy load?	A larger vehicle will enable us to transport the load.	Divide the load up into smaller units and make more than one trip.
If we started having some meetings then the communication problems in our company would be solved. *Re-state problem:* How can we solve the communication problems in our company?	Meetings will eliminate the communication problems in our company.	Restructure offices so people can see and speak to each other; hold social events to encourage interaction; give staff incentives to share problems and solutions.

Problem statement	The framed solution (the assumption)	Alternative solutions (challenges)
Our problem is that it takes us too long to deliver food to the tables so we can't attract more customers. *Re-state problem:* How can we attract more customers?	Delivering food quickly to the tables will attract more customers.	
We need to motivate slow employees. *Re-state problem:*	Motivating employees will stop them from being slow.	
Our problem is that we need more people behind the bar in order to take in more money. *Re-state problem:*	More employees behind the bar will generate more money.	

Make up your own problem statements:

1.

2.

Identify causes: the four Ps

The previous exercise showed how easy it is to frame a problem in terms of a single assumption or solution. This exercise encourages discrimination between symptom and cause.

Consider each problem statement and invent four possible causes of each. First consider each problem and re-state it if it contains a solution. Identify people causes, policy causes, procedure and plant causes. For example, the first one has been completed.

Problem	People	Policies	Procedures	Plant
Our workforce has low morale.	Executives act in oppressive ways.	Prevention of participation and inclusion.	Reporting processes too infrequent.	Over-crowding in offices.

Re-state problem:

We are not making profits because our managers are not cost conscious.

Re-state problem:

Problem	People	Policies	Procedures	Plant
We never have staff training because we don't have HR here.				
Re-state problem:				

The 'why' attack!

The purpose is to uncover your own assumptions, to appreciate small and big ideas and to help you think small and to think big. Tell someone about something you want e.g. 'I want a pay rise!' They will ask, 'Why'? You will say, 'Because I'm worth it'. They will ask, 'Why are you worth it?' You say, 'Because I work very hard'. 'Why?' 'Because I love my job.' 'Why?' 'Because I like the variety' etc. Soon they will run out of steam but you both will have uncovered assumptions and a string of connections. You've gone from a small request for more money to a big idea of job satisfaction. Now you need to see what the connection is—maybe you should pay the boss back some money for making you love your job so much! Use the form below to uncover possible solutions.

Problem	Why?

Our thinking is but star dust

Imagination is the highest kite you can fly.
—Lauren Bacall, actor

Life on earth depends on star cycles. Think about it. All the material on our planet comes from the interstellar medium created from the death of lots of stars. All the natural elements are produced in the cycles of stellar evolution. Every breath we take includes molecules that have existed since their creation by a star. The cycle of life *is* tied to the cycle of matter by a star and, ultimately, to the galaxy's evolution in which the stars live.

Our lives depend on the cycles of thinking that individuals engage in and how we act on that thinking. To think of it is to create it in the virtual world of our mind. Essentially, our thinking is derived from the star dust of the universe. Every thought we have includes basic building blocks of thought that have existed since their creation by other human beings. When people die, their thoughts live on in others and in the legacies they have left behind. Given the infinite variety of life, we can ask why certain pathways are consistently followed. Out of all the choices for nature and the universe to follow, why do we see the one we see? The answers to how our own pathway to life exists lie in this search.

Thinking in space–time

Imagine a very large ball. From a distance you can observe the ball in its three-dimensional space. If you were a miniature person living on the surface of the ball, however, you would think you were not on the surface of a ball but on a huge flat plane. This is exactly how human beings felt for millennia about the earth. Later in human history, the distances on our planet's sphere were travelled and carefully measured and we discovered that we are not living on a flat surface but on the curved surface of a large sphere.

Our thinking has developed like this over the centuries. On the surface we appear to be thinking in a flat dimension. But if we consciously consider the idea of the curvature of the surface of the ball we can adjust our whole way of thinking. Likewise, when we use all the keys of thinking critically we are experiencing the whole of space–time together. The way mathematicians prefer to define the surface of that sphere is to describe the entire sphere, not just a part of it. Similarly, critical thinkers who are catalysts, poets and creators prefer to describe the whole of the experience the whole of the time.

My experience is that we are moving in very defined space and time environments that limit our thinking. The categories we create in our conversations, the labels we are taught to use at home and in school, and the language we invent set the parameters for interpreting our reality. When you catch yourself using particular language and categorising experiences with these words then you have acknowledged some hidden assumptions. This is a step in the right direction of further illuminating your thought environments. The way we come to prefer to say things in a particular way and then the way we prefer to behave are all choices about our personal and social time and space. Our preferences make us who we are and how we think.

It is not possible to escape interpreting our perceptions in terms of categories. As humans we are inevitably categorical! Through categories we create our reality and the way we interpret reality. Can you see the irony in the following statement? There are two kinds of people in this world, those who put everything into two groups and those who do not. Well, this statement has just put things into two categories! What criteria do you use to judge into which group things are allocated: alive/dead; good/bad; male/female; easy to count/hard to count; likes/dislikes; soft/hard; profitable/ unprofitable? People have their own preferences and these determine what they practise. What people practise is what they become proficient at. Preference leads to practices which lead to proficiencies.

Invitation to reflect critically

My exploration of thinking critically may seem prescriptive— telling you to do certain things so you will become a master of thinking critically. My purpose, however, is not to provide advice but to lead you into a sincere reflection and exploration of the topic in the hope that together we will deepen our understanding of the field. Giving advice is risky and following it can be foolish. Do things because *you* want to, because *you* see potential value for yourself and for the *greater good*.

You might think this suggestion is one of commonsense and you might also infer from this that you should not do things you do not want to do, that everything you do should be because you want to and because you see there will be a benefit. This may even seem absurd and impossible to follow because we can all easily catch ourselves doing things we do not want to do and things we are convinced have no likely benefit. Positives can also be found in the things we do not want to do, they can benefit us if approached appropriately. So, how are we to judge then when we should do something, such as allowing yourself the time to read this book?

In this book I am inviting you to enhance your mental capacity, to see the invisible in what you are used to looking at every day. When you say 'yes' to this invitation, when you decide to act, and when you do actually act, you will enter a different world. When I suggest you do certain activities and that you sharpen your observation skills, that you try to notice things you see everyday in a different way and that you identify and question the things you take for granted I am simply inviting you to think differently, to think critically.

Thinking critically is about the careful consideration of all the issues possible and knowing the difference between simplicity and complexity. The difference between simplicity and complexity is a matter of being able to perceive a situation from different points of view. An examination of the seemingly absurd, of complexity itself, of what we see before us in a new way is what I am suggesting you do. What I am encouraging is for you to think carefully first, act second, reflect on your actions and then think again, trying to make a different sense of your experience.

Drawing a new map

In our everyday thinking we follow our own personal maps of reality, but these maps only symbolise the territory. A map is simply a description and an explanation of something. All of them are a sketch or picture of what is real. A map is what we draw of what we think of the territory. When you think about an issue your thinking is simply *your* own perception, *your* interpretation and *your* understanding of it. No one else will have exactly the same version that you do.

Your own thinking is only one perspective. Although your map probably works well for you, there are other perspectives that may work better for others. There can be many maps of the same territory that are different from each other. Diversity is the essence of emphasis. Each map or each way of thinking about reality is unique. Each map will highlight particular aspects. Through sharing our maps—for example, through team work and cooperation—we are able to update and change our maps as we want to, thus avoiding the likelihood of becoming stagnant in our thinking.

Thinking critically is a way of creating different maps of reality.

To continue the analogy of the map, your new map—your map of thinking critically—will take you on a journey that follows new paths. Thinking critically is stimulated by a sense of adventure and discovery as much as it is by a sense of dissatisfaction with the way things are. To some, the path forward may cause some fear and worry. You may worry about losing yourself. This is natural—after all, you are challenging the foundations of your beliefs. However, it's worth remembering, too, that to not take up the challenge to venture out will also cause you to lose yourself. Challenge is a healthy thing because it allows you to know yourself much better than you already do.

A three-step process

1. Start to question the way you think and feel—your assumptions. You could begin by asking yourself, What am I feeling? Why am I feeling this way? Why am I thinking these things?
2. Discard the methods you are comfortable with. For example, if you're in the habit of writing everything down, stop doing that and rely more on your memory. Can you imagine what might happen if you try to develop a different way? You will upset the balance within yourself but the reward will be greater flexibility in your approach. To improve your memory try and fix things in your mind in vivid pictures with motion and colour.
3. Generate new ways of thinking and feeling. How do you do this? By using your imagination. Blocks to thinking critically are really blocks to exploring and using your imagination in ways you have not done before. There's no trick to developing your imagination. You simply need to try to be yourself, your authentic self, without pressure to conform to peer group pressure or expectations of a culture designed for a group rather than for a particular individual. You could try to identify things you haven't thought about before. Ask yourself how you can start to think about them. How do you feel about trying to find new ways of feeling? What would it mean to feel in ways you are not accustomed to? Can you try to *appreciate* feelings in another person that have puzzled you?

Using the imagination

There's no limit to the imagination. Anybody can create vivid, colourful, motion-filled images of what could be. Let your mind go and think crazy thoughts. Experiment! The secrets of creativity are locked in what we actually see, not in what we do not see. Creativity is locked within our senses and within our intuition. To fantasise and produce unreal images is a key to unlocking creativity. By paying extra attention to what is before us *and* what is within us we increase our capacity to think differently.

Having trouble? Useful metaphors for creativity are 'wind' and 'water'. We can't see the wind but we can feel it on our face and see its effects when trees sway, clouds shift, clothes flutter, so it reminds us to pay attention to what is within us, what we can't see. We can only see the effects of what is within us when we pay attention to our actions, just as we can only see wind when we notice its action. Water is visible and it represents all the things we can observe outside ourselves.

Imagination embraces big ideas—for example, the notion that there are multiple parallel universes. Thinking about the fact that we live in a vast reality rather than a tiny space gives a new dimension to what it means to be human.

Imagination can turn a failed idea into something useful. It can re-define 'failure' to 'work-in-progress'. Instead of giving up when a new type of glue failed to stick anything together permanently, Arthur Fry and Spencer Silver came up with the idea of Post-it Notes, those little paper notes that can be temporarily put on and pulled off things several times over. Out of failure a new useful invention was born.

The story of Post-it Notes resulted from a synergy between two people who were in search of different yet complementary solutions. Arthur Fry, 3M corporate scientist and inventor, was looking for a type of bookmark that would not fall out or damage his church hymnals. His colleague at 3M, Dr Spencer Silver, had developed a failed glue that was strong enough to stick to surfaces gently and could be repositioned without leaving any residue. Fry got the idea that if he applied some of Silver's adhesive to the edge of a piece of paper it could be used in the church hymnals without damaging them. Soon the realisation came that this mobile bookmark had other potential functions, to communicate details and to organise work. It took several years of marketing by 3M to make the Post-it

Note a household name with widespread use. My editor sent me this manuscript literally littered with Post-it Notes with queries I had to deal with. Like it or not, Post-it Notes impact on everyone even if you try to avoid them!

This is where tenacity and optimism come in. If you try to open a business and it fails, and then you try a different way and that fails and again you try a third way and that, too, fails, you might be forgiven for thinking your business idea is a complete failure. But what you have done is to learn three different ways of how *not* to set up that business. Now you can begin again with that knowledge as a solid base behind you. The idea is to make all the mistakes first and learn what doesn't work so you can get on with what *does* work.

Concluding remarks

I have written the book both from a desire to deepen my own understanding, to grasp a deeper appreciation of the nature and place of thinking critically in work and life, and to uncover the main lines of all there is to be understood on this topic. But our world is extraordinarily complex and the attitudes we experience are similarly many, dynamic and complex. Complexity can be confusing and threatening because it is not neat, tidy and simple, and people prefer simplicity.

People tend to ignore the many possibilities open to them because they like to hear that there are two ways, the right and the wrong way. Frequently, one way turns out to be the accepted way that subsequently becomes the habitual and ordinary way. People, however, want excellence and want to receive recognition for doing their best and perhaps being the best. People begin the search for 'best practice'. When we find it we try to adopt it so we can become excellent. But very soon the context changes. We are slow to change out practice so that what we continue to do then becomes ordinary again and the search for the extraordinary eventually begins over. We use the same cycle; we start hunting for exemplary practice by people who can show us the right way. But people should not resign themselves to flat double-dimensional life, where one dimension is an escape from another that only occurs rarely. Every experience has within it a bias that we should come to appreciate. Whatever the present looks and feels like we should delight in it.

Those who espouse two ways and promote only one tend to become recognised as the great teachers. They save people from further confusion, from bewildering complexity and from making hard choices. They often offer single choices that are easy to make because if you do not you will be a failure and perhaps you will not survive. The actual making of the choice is easy, and celebrating the making of the right choice is pleasant, but some attitudes will not make it so easy or pleasant to implement the actions that flow from the choice. Often the wisdom of excellence offers simplicity in choice. However, simplicity is not always wisdom, as the best choices are imbued with their own inner complexity and dynamism.

Solutions to problems exist in the perceptions and realities we co-create. The difficulty we experience is the identification of solutions and the making of choices. Any one choice is always a choice of not doing something else; one way of perceiving is also a way of not perceiving. Openness to perspectives and a diligent search for difference will serve us well. It is the differences that make us unique while our similarities bind us, give us an identity and a common sense of purpose and strategy. Every person is always like all other people in most ways; we are always like some other people in some ways, and we are like no other people in just a few ways. It is these few differences that make the difference and become the focus of learning in communities and in organisations. The importance of difference is summarised well by Walter Lippmann: *Where all think alike, no one thinks very much.* Communities of inquiry and communities that practise together are distinguished by a valuing of difference, by an openness to exploration and challenge, and by a constant desire for renewal and regeneration.

Our capacity to be on the never-ending quest of thinking in better ways can only improve our own life and the lives of others.

Index

Index